HIS STORY

(Volume 3)

A Simple Look at

THE BOOK OF ACTS

With Outlines of

THE NEW TESTAMENT LETTERS

Carmel Carberry

www.gardenlandministries.uk

www.carmelcarberry.com

Produced by Amazon Digital Services
ISBN: 9781973767565

All Photos/Images by John & Carmel Carberry and family
Special thanks to Matt Carberry for photo at waterfall
(Used with permission / All rights reserved)

As always, thanks to all who support me while writing, Carmel x

PLEASE NOTE: With reference to Timelines / Dates of Bible Books and Events: all dates offered are approximate and subject to information available at the time of writing.

Dedicated to

Ronald Frederick Rumsey

Author's Note

Over the years, many people have told me that they find The Bible difficult to read, and that often they do not understand it. Yet there is such wonderful wisdom and wise counsel within its pages.

With this in mind, I hope that this series will help readers to understand a bit more from the wealth of knowledge that The Scriptures contain and begin to enjoy them.

I pray that this insight helps readers to know deeper The One whom The Bible points to: The God of Love who is seen through His Son Jesus, who came for you.

CONTENTS

In the Old Testament,
God promised to pour out His Spirit
and make 'rivers flow' on barren heights;
He promised to make 'springs of water'
flow in valleys, and turn 'deserts
into pools of water'.

In the New Testament,
God fulfilled His promise by pouring
out His Spirit at Pentecost (Acts 2);
and 'like a river' The Holy Spirit
continues to flow, for all
people to receive.

Related scriptures: Is 41:18 / Is 44:3
Joel 2:28 / Acts 2:1-4,15-18

God pours out showers of blessing to refresh you
(from Acts 3:19b)

SIMPLE OVERVIEW OF THE BIBLE

The OLD TESTAMENT consists of the first 39 books of The Bible. The name 'Testament' refers to a covenant (meaning a 'binding agreement' or 'promise') that has been made between God and man.

In the Old Testament, we see that God made promises to men of faith who lived long ago; and God remains faithful to His promises *(for example: Adam ~ Genesis 1:26-30 // Noah ~ Genesis 9:11 // Abraham ~ Genesis 12:1-3 // Moses ~ Exodus 19-24 // David ~ 2 Samuel 5:7)*

The Bible begins by telling us that God is the Creator of all life and the whole universe. It introduces us to the first human beings and their descendants, with an emphasis on Abraham, his son Isaac, and his grandson Jacob.... who fathered the nation Israel.

Then the story of the Israelites' exodus from Egypt is told, and the development of Israel as a nation, including a variety of laws that were given to them.

There are also accounts of Leaders and Kings who ruled over the people and the many up and downs that this small but enduring nation faced over the centuries.

God spoke through many prophets to this nation with guidance, encouragements, and warnings, but also gave a message for the whole world through them that He would send an eternal Saviour who would come for all mankind.

The Bible as a whole shows mankind's need for a Saviour, and it prophesies about Him throughout the Old Testament.

Many rituals in the Old Testament (OT) have symbolism attached to them that act as a pointer towards the promised 'Christ' (*meaning 'Anointed One'*). Many of the Biblical heroes are also like 'types' or 'shadows' that point to Him.

~~~~~~~

Jesus is The Christ who is revealed in the New Testament (NT).
Some Bible references to consider: Isaiah 9:6 (OT) //
Matthew 1:23 / Matt 22:36-40 / Rom 10:4 (NT)

~~~~~~~

The NEW TESTAMENT is composed of the remaining 27 books of The Bible.

As we saw previously, the name 'Testament' refers to a covenant (agreement or promise) made between God and man. Ultimately, the fulfilment of all the Old Testament laws and prophets has come through Jesus *(Matt 5:17).*

The New Testament shows us the NEW COVENANT, which is the Eternal Covenant of Grace that God has made through the complete and finished work of Jesus at The Cross, and by His Resurrection *(Rom 3:23-26 / Heb 1:1-3).*

The New Testament tells us how Jesus accomplished salvation for all mankind and showed us God's Heart *(John 1:18).* We see the Love and Grace of God revealed in His Life and Ministry, as shown in The Gospels (Matthew, Mark, Luke, and John).

Then the New Testament pages tell us about the pouring out of God's Holy Spirit, the growth and impact of the early church (Acts) and records letters written by The Apostles to encourage and instruct the early church, and the generations that followed.

We can glean great wisdom, encouragement and insight through all of these, which lead us to 'Good News' ~ The Revelation of God's Love and Grace through Christ, God's One and Only Son *(John 3:16-17)*

~~~~~~~

Following the introduction, Sections 1-3 offer a simple look through the Book of Acts. It shows the pouring out of The Holy Spirit, and how The Apostles share the Good News of Jesus in Jerusalem; in Judea and Samaria; and leading to the whole world (Acts 1:8)

Sections 4-5 offer a simple outline of The New Testament Letters, which were written by The Apostles to the churches of the time. Studying these Bible books can help us in our lives today.

Sections 6-7 offer reference lists, with notes relating to The Person of The Holy Spirit (who continues to help us). A list of Bible Symbolism (simplified) is also included to offer some insight into prophetic writing found in The Bible.

The end pages offer information about Gardenland, concluding with encouragements and prayer to bless the reader.

~~~~~~~

INTRODUCTION TO THE BOOK OF ACTS

'ACTS' is considered to have been written around 67 AD. It is the second letter written by Luke to a man named 'Theophilus' (believed to have been a Roman Government Officer). Luke's first letter is the book we know today as 'The Gospel of Luke'.

> *Luke 1:1-4 / Acts 1:1-2*
> *Many people have set out to write accounts about the events that have been fulfilled among us. They used the eyewitness reports circulating among us from the early disciples. Having carefully investigated everything from the beginning, I also have decided to write an accurate account for you, most honorable Theophilus, so you can be certain of the truth of everything you were taught...*
> *In my first book I told you, Theophilus, about everything Jesus began to do and teach until the day He was taken up to heaven after giving His chosen apostles further instructions through the Holy Spirit.*

Acts tells us about the outpouring of God's Spirit on the followers of Jesus after His ascension to Heaven (Acts 1-2), and how His Spirit empowered the believers to spread God's Message about Christ.

In Acts chapters 1-7 we see the Apostle Peter and his fellow believers begin to preach to Jewish people in and around Jerusalem. In chapters 8-12 we see the Apostle Philip and his fellow believers take the Good News of Jesus to Judea and Samaria. In chapters 13-28 we see The Apostle Paul take the Gospel to the Gentiles as he takes 'Missionary Trips' to other nations, which ultimately is still spreading the message to the world today.

The final chapter of Acts records an account of Paul being under arrest in Rome and awaiting trial (Acts 28:17-31). With this in mind, there is a compelling belief that Luke's writing was to provide a background history to Theophilus, the Governmental Official who represented Paul at his trial.

The aim of Luke's letters appear to be to inform Theophilus of events prior to Paul's arrest, to help give evidence in support of Paul's innocence under Roman law. Today, the Book of Acts offers the reader a special insight into how The Church began.

A group of frightened believers (who were in prayer but hiding from the authorities) became bold witnesses for Jesus, when the promised Holy Spirit (Joel 2:28 / Acts 1:8) came upon them at Pentecost (Acts 2).

Empowered by God's Spirit, these people (often weak and uneducated) went on to preach with miraculous signs and wonders following them. Despite desperate trials and persecution, the believers grew in great numbers. And they continued to speak His 'Message of Reconciliation' to all who would listen (2 Cor 5:17-21).

This message continues to go out today ~ to ALL people, in ALL nations ~ 'to the ends of the earth' (Acts 1:8)

So many people are looking for God, all over the world, in many different ways. 'Acts' tells us that Jesus came for everyone, both Jew and Gentile (non-Jew) everywhere, across all time. And God's Holy Spirit has been given to help, guide and teach us. All of this is by God's Grace and Mercy, given freely, as we look to His Son.

Some related verses of encouragement

Joel 2:28-29
I will pour out My Spirit upon all people...your sons and daughters will prophesy...I will pour out My Spirit on men and women alike.

(Note: Joel 2:28 is an Old Testament promise that was quoted by Peter in Acts 2:17)

John 1:12 / Romans 8:14
..To all who believed Him (Jesus) and accepted Him, He gave the right to become children of God....for all who are led by the Spirit of God are children of God.

2 Corinthians 5:17-21
...Anyone who belongs to Christ has become a new person. The old life is gone; a new life has begun! ... All of this is a gift from God, who brought us back to Himself through Christ... For God was in Christ, reconciling the world to Himself, no longer counting people's sins against them. And He gave us this wonderful message of reconciliation.

.... So we are Christ's ambassadors; God is making His appeal through us.... For God made Christ, who never sinned, to be the offering for our sin, so that we could be made right with God through Christ.

Romans 15:13
I pray that God, the source of hope, will fill you completely with joy and peace because you trust in Him. Then you will overflow with confident hope through the power of the Holy Spirit.

- WORD OF ENCOURAGEMENT
(from The Fathers Heart)

I promised from ancient times to pour out My Spirit on all mankind, and to give My blessing to every man, woman, and child in all nations across the earth.

My Promise is being fulfilled ~ My Spirit descended on The Day of Pentecost and He is present today. He lives within the hearts of all who trust in Jesus.

I sent forth My Spirit to comfort and guide people into all truth. Therefore, take heart all you who hope in God. I have not forgotten you.

I have fulfilled My Promise, and through My Spirit I will work all things together for good, as you pray and seek Me first in your life.

I AM with you, always. I dwell in your heart by the power of My Spirit, and in the Love of My Son. I will never leave you.

For Bible Study (if desired)
Ps 27:14 / Is 44:3 / Joel 2:28-29 / Matt 28:19-20
John 3:16-17 / John 14:16 / John 16:13-14 / Acts 2:1-4
Acts 2:17+39 / Acts 10:45 / Rom 8:28 / 2 Cor 1:20-22
Gal 4:6 / Heb 6:10 / Heb 10:10 / Heb 13:5
Eph 1:13-14 / / Eph 2:18-22 / 1 John 2:2

JESUS ASCENDS TO HEAVEN; THE HOLY SPRIT IS POURED OUT; THE CHURCH IS BORN

A SIMPLE LOOK AT CHAPTERS 1-8

Acts 1:8
Jesus told His Disciples: you will receive power when the Holy Spirit comes upon you. And you will be My witnesses, telling people about Me everywhere—IN JERUSALEM, throughout Judea, in Samaria, and to the ends of the earth."

A SIMPLE OVERVIEW OF ACTS CHAPTERS 1-12

Jesus speaks with His Disciples, then returns to Heaven

In Acts Chapter 1, Luke reminds the reader of the resurrection of Christ, and then presents an account of Jesus talking with His Disciples.

Within this conversation, Jesus reassures His friends that God's promise to send The Holy Spirit will be fulfilled, then He ascends to Heaven before their eyes.

Angels appear to those watching to proclaim that one day Jesus will return in the same way that His friends saw Him leave. As the chapter goes on, we read that Matthias is chosen to replace Judas.

There were a number of religious festivals celebrated throughout the year in the Jewish calendar. People from near and far would travel to the city to join in these celebrations, including from other nations.

One of these festivals is 'Shavuot' ~ known as the 'Feast of Weeks' or the 'Feast of 50 days' ~ which was established in Jewish history (Old Testament chapters for reference: Exodus 23,34; Leviticus 23; Deuteronomy 26).

It is also known as 'Pentecost' (derived from the Greek word meaning '50') and in relation to our western calendar took place around May-June.

Pentecost

In Acts Chapter 2, we see that at the time of this festival, The Disciples and other believers were staying at a house in Jerusalem, when The Holy Spirit poured out upon them.

As the believers gathered together to pray, The Holy Spirit came upon them and 'tongues of fire' appeared over them. They began to speak in a multitude of languages (tongues) that they had never learned and did not know how to speak naturally.

> *Acts 2:1-4 (GNT)*
> *When the day of Pentecost came, all the believers were gathered together in one place. Suddenly there was a noise from the sky which sounded like a strong wind blowing, and it filled the whole house where they were sitting. Then they saw what looked like tongues of fire which spread out and touched each person there. They were all filled with the Holy Spirit and began to talk in other languages, as the Spirit enabled them to speak.*

As the believers continued to praise God in various languages with great boldness, people in the city could hear the sound of the rejoicing. Visitors to the city heard their own language being spoken among the throng of voices, and the people became curious at the incredible sound.

As the people gathered closer to listen, The Apostle Peter stood up and addressed the crowd. He preached with wisdom and power, and explained prophesies from the Old Testament and how they pointed to Jesus.

About three thousand people came to believe in Jesus that day having heard this one 'sermon' telling the Good News of mankind reconciled to God through His Son.

Dedication of the believers

As the believers continued to meet together, they dedicated themselves to the teaching of The Apostles, prayed and 'broke bread' (also known as 'Eucharist' / 'The Lord's Supper' / 'Holy Communion' in churches today ~ Luke 22:19-20). They sold possessions and freely gave to those who had need.

Signs and wonders followed them

When The Apostles preached God's Word, they also performed signs and wonders, and the number of believers grew daily.

In Acts Chapter 3, we see Peter and John on their way to The Temple in Jerusalem, to pray. When they got there, they healed a lame man who was begging at the temple gate. The people in The Temple were amazed as they saw the man walking and began to ask questions.

So, Peter again preached with power and authority, telling those that gathered that Jesus is The Messiah and that He is The One who healed through them.

As we move into Acts Chapter 4, we see that the Religious Leaders of the day did not understand the events so arrested Peter and John, and put them in jail. However, many people believed the message The Apostles spoke, and The Church grew to around five thousand people.

Boldness in the face of persecution

When Peter and John were questioned about the events, they spoke with boldness from The Holy Spirit. The Religious Leaders were astonished by uneducated men speaking with such knowledge and wisdom. They also looked upon the man who had been healed in wonder.

On their release, Peter and John met with the believers to pray together, and they were again filled with the Holy Spirit. Despite the authorities call for The Apostles to stop preaching about the resurrection of Christ, they continued to share The Good News.

God's Grace was with them as they spoke with power, authority, and boldness. The believers were of one heart and mind, and shared everything they had. From this place of unity, they brought money from the sales of houses and land to The Apostles to share according to the need.

Spiritual battle

Sometimes we can read difficult passages in The Bible. Even the most mature Christian needs to pray for revelation, so it's prudent to ask God for wisdom to help us understand and to consider the context of the passage we are reading.

> *James 1:5*
> *If you need wisdom, ask our generous God, and he will give it to you. He will not rebuke you for asking.*

With that in mind, Acts Chapter 5 begins with a challenging passage….

….But it shows us that our Heavenly Father sees beyond any outward display of piety coming from a sense of self-righteousness. ***God sees the heart***; He sees when there is genuine motivation, genuine love, and genuine dependence on Him.

Deception exposed

In Acts Chapter 5, we read about two people who pretended to bring all of the profit from the sale of their land and possessions, when they were not required to do so (Acts 5:4). Although it appeared a 'religious act', the scriptures reveal a malevolent source behind the deceit.

> *Acts 5:3 (NLV)*
> *Peter said to Ananias, "Why did you let Satan fill your heart?*

Ananias and Sapphira were both offered the chance of repentance but chose to maintain their lie to The Apostles and to God Himself. Peter was given a word of knowledge (from The Holy Spirit) of the events that this couple were about to bring upon themselves. But they continued with the deceit which overwhelmed the couple, with tragic consequences.

> *1 Sam 6:17*
> *The LORD does not look at the things people look at. People look at the outward appearance, but the LORD looks at the heart.*

Sometimes a spiritual battle can be taking place during some of the difficult circumstances we encounter. If we discern this to be so, then we need to recognise that, ***through faith in Christ,*** we are able to stand against the spiritual enemy and overcome.

James 4:7 (AMP) / 1 John 2:14
Submit to the authority of God. Resist the devil [stand firm against him] and he will flee from you.... God's word lives in your hearts...you have won your battle with the evil one.

Godly respect, deliverance, and healing

As we move on in Acts Chapter 5, we see that a renewed reverence for God develops among the people and a great respect for The Apostles. We also see that any who were oppressed by evil were set free and the sick were healed, as the Apostles performed great signs and wonders.

Persecution also came from Religious Authorities. The Apostles were arrested and put in jail once again. However, an Angel came and released The Apostles from their confinement, so that they could continue to preach about the New Life that God offers to ALL through Jesus.

Acts 5:19-21 / John 3:16-17 (NIV)
...During the night an angel of the Lord opened the doors of the jail and brought them out. "Go, stand in the temple courts," he said, "and tell the people all about this new life. "At daybreak they entered the temple courts, as they had been told, and began to teach the people...For God so loved the world that He gave His one and only Son, that whoever believes in Him shall not perish but have eternal life. For God did not send His Son into the world to condemn the world, but to save the world through Him.

When the guards were sent to check the jail they found it locked and secure, and yet The Apostles were not there. Upon finding them in The Temple courts preaching, they were escorted away by the guards and brought to stand before the Religious Leaders once again.

Good News cannot be silenced

Peter spoke with boldness about the events that had occurred, and shared The Good News of Jesus.

One of The Leaders then persuaded the others to let The Apostles go. But they were flogged before their release and were instructed again (by the authorities) to stop preaching. The Apostles went on their way rejoicing, and continued to preach The Gospel and heal the sick as God told them.

> *From Acts 5:12-15 (AMP)*
> *At the hands of the apostles many signs and wonders (attesting miracles) were continually taking place among the people. And by common consent they all met together [at the temple]....the people were holding them in high esteem and were speaking highly of them.*
>
> *More and more believers in the Lord, crowds of men and women, were constantly being added to their number, to such an extent that they even carried their sick out into the streets...so that when Peter came by at least his shadow might fall on one of them [with healing power].*
>
> *Acts 5:42 (NIV)*
> *Day after day, in the temple courts and from house to house, they never stopped teaching and proclaiming the good news that Jesus is the Messiah.*

Food distribution / faith and miracles

Acts 6 begins by telling us that the number of believers were increasing rapidly. It goes on to say that some discontent developed when a group of believers felt their widows missed out during a food delivery.

After talking with all of the groups, The Apostles appointed seven men to be responsible for the distribution of food, including a man called Stephen who was 'full of faith and the Holy Spirit' (Acts 5:5). Stephen performed miracles among the people by God's power and grace, and many more people came to believe, including Jewish priests.

> *Acts 6:8 (TLB)*
> *Stephen, the man so full of faith and the Holy Spirit's power [full of grace and truth] did spectacular miracles among the people.*

One day some men began to debate with Stephen but they could not fault what he said. Since they could not stand against his wisdom, the men instead persuaded some people to lie about him to stir up trouble.

This led to Stephen being arrested and brought before the authorities, where false witnesses gave their accusations. But Stephen's face appeared to shine and looked like the 'face of an angel' (Acts 6:15).

Forgiveness in the face of persecution

In Acts Chapter 7, we see that when Stephen was called to answer the allegations, he went on to preach to all who had gathered there. He recited the nation's history and how it led to the coming of Christ.

He spoke about Jesus paying for all sin at The Cross, rising from the dead and ascending into Heaven. Stephen urged his listeners not to reject the message of hope for all people through faith in God's Son.

Then Stephen began to look up and saw a vision of Heaven, and went on to tell his accusers how he saw 'Jesus standing at the Right Hand of God'.

Those who heard this were infuriated, and dragged him out of the city to be stoned. Even then, Stephen prayed for ***God to forgive them.*** The accusers laid their coats down at the feet of a young man named 'Saul' as they proceeded to kill Stephen (who became the first Christian martyr).

From Acts 7:59-60 (NLT)
Stephen prayed, "Lord Jesus, receive my spirit." He fell to his knees, shouting, "Lord, don't charge them with this sin!"

TO CONSIDER:

When we reflect on the teaching of Jesus in The Gospels, we can be assured that Stephen, along with believers from across all time who have gone before us, now stand victorious in God's Eternal Presence.

They are an example to us today: to keep our eyes on Christ, to persevere, act in faith, forgive and don't give up. Despite earthly troubles, our Heavenly Father wants to give us hope and reassure us that we have a future, here and in eternity.

Please see related Bible promises shown on following page.

SOME BIBLE PROMISES TO ENCOURAGE
especially in times of difficulties

Word spoken by Jesus in The Gospels *(personalised)*

From John 10:28-30 (NIV)
"I give YOU eternal life, and you shall never perish; no one will snatch you out of My hand. My Father is greater than all; no one can snatch you out of My Father's hand. I and the Father are one."

Written by The Apostles in The New Testament Letters:

From Hebrews 12:1-2a (GNT)
As for us, we have this large crowd of witnesses around us. So then, let us rid ourselves of everything that gets in the way, and of the sin which holds on to us so tightly, and let us run with determination the race that lies before us. Let us keep our eyes fixed on Jesus, on whom our faith depends from beginning to end.

From 1 Peter 1:3-5 (The Message)
What a God we have! And how fortunate we are to have Him....Because Jesus was raised from the dead, we've been given a brand-new life and have everything to live for, including a future in heaven—and the future starts now! God is keeping careful watch over us and the future. The Day is coming when you'll have it all—life healed and whole!

The message of Jesus is one of hope, strength, and encouragement. It is a gift from The Fathers Heart for every person of every nation (across all time).

Section Two

THE MESSAGE OF JESUS IS TAKEN BEYOND JERUSALEM AND REACHES MORE PEOPLE

A SIMPLE LOOK AT ACTS CHAPTERS 8-12

Acts 1:8
Jesus told His Disciples: you will receive power when the Holy Spirit comes upon you. And you will be My witnesses, telling people about Me everywhere—in Jerusalem, THROUGHOUT JUDEA, IN SAMARIA, and to the ends of the earth."

The Church scattered

As we move into Acts chapter 8, we read that the Church entered a time of great persecution in the city of Jerusalem, which caused all except The Apostles to be scattered across Judea and Samaria.

The man named Saul began to have Christians put into prison in an attempt to stop the growth of The Church and the spread of The Gospel ('Good News of Christ').

However, despite the terrible things that had happened, the believers who were scattered preached The Word wherever they went, and The Gospel spread even further.

When Philip preached about Jesus in a city in Samaria, the crowds listened and believed, then many were healed and delivered from evil spirits.

There was a man there named 'Simon' who had tricked the people for some time, boasting about himself and practicing sorcery. But after believing the message about Christ, Simon repented and was baptised, along with many others in the city.

Peter and John arrived to pray for the new believers and that they would receive the Holy Spirit. As the people were filled with the power of God's Spirit, Simon offered money to the Apostles to 'buy the power' he witnessed.

Peter rejected Simons offer and told him to repent. The Holy Spirit is a ***free gift of God's Grace*** for all who ask and receive. Then Simon asked for forgiveness and prayer.

Luke 11:10-13 (The Message)
"Don't bargain with God. Be direct. Ask for what you need. This is not a cat-and-mouse, hide-and-seek game we're in. If your little boy asks for a serving of fish, do you scare him with a live snake on his plate? If your little girl asks for an egg, do you trick her with a spider?
...you wouldn't think of such a thing...And don't you think the Father who conceived you in love will give the Holy Spirit when you ask him?"

The Apostles then continued to preach to all the villages, as they made their way home to Jerusalem.

Philip preaches to an Ethiopian

Later, The Holy Spirit led Philip to walk down a road where a man was travelling in a carriage. The man was an Ethiopian eunuch, and was reading from 'Isaiah' (a book in The Old Testament). As God's Spirit led him, Philp walked beside the carriage and began to talk with the man.

Acts 8:26-29
As for Philip, an angel of the Lord said to him, "Go south down the desert road that runs from Jerusalem to Gaza." So he started out, and he met the treasurer of Ethiopia, a eunuch of great authority under the Kandake, the queen of Ethiopia.

The eunuch had gone to Jerusalem to worship, and he was now returning. Seated in his carriage, he was reading aloud from the book of the prophet Isaiah. The Holy Spirit said to Philip, "Go over and walk along beside the carriage."

During their conversation, Philip explained to the man that the passage he was reading *(Isaiah 53, in The Old Testament)* was a prophecy about Jesus.

As they travelled further, they came to some water and the man asked to be baptised. Both Philip and the man went under the water, and as they came up, The Holy Spirit took Philip on to his next location.

The man went on his way rejoicing. Philip then appeared at a place called 'Azotuz' (Ashdod) and preached in all the towns until he reached Caesarea.

Saul turns to Jesus

In Acts chapter 9, Saul has an incredible encounter with the Risen Christ. Saul was travelling to Damascus to deliver letters to the synagogues to request that if he were to find any followers of 'The Way', then he would be allowed to take them back to Jerusalem as prisoners.

However, as he nears Damascus, a Great Light shone from Heaven all around him and he fell to the ground in awe. He heard a voice from The Light speak to him, saying "I AM Jesus whom you are persecuting".

Saul's companions only heard the sound but stood amazed. Then they helped Paul to continue his journey (as he could not see after the event).

> *Acts 9:3-9 (NCV)*
> *As he neared Damascus on his journey, suddenly a light from heaven flashed around him. He fell to the ground and heard a voice say to him, "Saul, Saul, why do you persecute me?" "Who are you, Lord?" Saul asked.*

"I am Jesus, whom you are persecuting," he replied. "Now get up and go into the city, and you will be told what you must do." The men traveling with Saul stood there speechless; they heard the sound but did not see anyone. Saul got up from the ground, but when he opened his eyes he could see nothing. So they led him by the hand into Damascus. For three days he was blind, and did not eat or drink anything.

A disciple of Jesus called Ananias lived in Damascus. God spoke to him in a vision and called on him to go to the house where Saul was praying. The Lord then told Ananias to lay his hands on Saul and heal him (to restore his sight).

The disciple was perplexed and began to recount the persecution that followers of Jesus received at the hands of Saul. But God again instructed Ananias to go, and said that He would lead Saul to become someone who would proclaim The Gospel to all nations.

Ananias followed The Lord's instructions, prayed for Saul to be healed and to be filled with the Holy Spirit. In an instant, something which looked like 'scales' fell from Saul's eyes and he could see.

Saul got up, was baptised, and began to eat and drink to regain his strength. He then went on to spend several days with the disciples in Damascus and began to preach in the synagogues. He preached that Jesus is The Son of God which astonished his hearers.

Acts 9:22
Saul's preaching became more and more powerful, and the Jews in Damascus couldn't refute his proofs that Jesus was indeed the Messiah.

Saul is persecuted

After a while, a conspiracy was spread about Saul, which incited some in the community to try to kill him. Recognising this, friends of Saul helped him to escape by lowering him in a basket over the city wall during the night.

Saul went to Jerusalem to join with believers there, but they were afraid of him and did not believe he had really changed. However, Barnabas took him to meet The Apostles and explained to them all that had taken place.

Saul stayed with them and preached in Jerusalem until he encountered further threats on his life. When the believers found out about the threats, they took Paul to Caesarea and sent him from there to Tarsus (to protect him).

> *Taken from Acts 9:31 (AMP)*
> *The church throughout Judea, Galilee and Samaria enjoyed a time without persecution, being built up in wisdom, virtue, and faith. They walked in the 'fear of the Lord' (the 'reverence of God'). With comfort and encouragement from the Holy Spirit, the church continued to grow in numbers.*

Peter, Aeneas, and Dorcas

As Peter continued to travel around the country, he visited a place called Lydda. There he met a man named Aeneas and healed him of paralysis. When the people in Lydda and Sharon saw the man walking, they turned to God.

A believer named Dorcas (also known as Tabitha) lived in a place called Joppa (near Lydda). She was known for helping the poor in her area.

When Peter heard that Dorcas has suddenly died, he went to visit where her friends had laid her. Her friends were all wailing with grief so he sent them out of the room, kneeled and prayed.

Then he spoke to her saying “Tabitha, get up”. She opened her eyes and Peter helped her to her feet. As the people saw the miracle, many more believed and turned to Jesus. After this, Peter stayed in Joppa for a time with a tanner named Simon.

Cornelius and Peter

In Acts chapter 10, we read about a man named Cornelius whose faith, and that of his whole family and household, were recognised by God.

> **Encouragement note:**
> This story is an encouragement to all who may not feel confident, and might not always feel that they are understood by other people. The Bible shows that **God knows when you trust in Him** and that **He sent Jesus for you** [John 3:16-17). **He loves you and knows you by name**. { Isaiah 43:1 confirms, ‘The LORD who created you says, "Do not be afraid--I will save you. I have called you by name" }

One day an angel appeared to Cornelius in a vision, telling him that God heard his prayers and saw the kindness he showed to people.

The angel told Cornelius about the house where Peter was staying, and instructed him to send for Peter to come to speak to him, and his family and household (about Christ).

While his men were traveling to bring the message to Peter, the Apostle was praying on the roof of Simon’s house.

As Peter prayed, he too had a vision where God spoke to him to prepare him for the upcoming visit.

God spoke to Peter in a form that he could relate to. In a vision (using 'picture language') He showed Peter types of food that he would normally reject because his religious beliefs considered them 'unclean'. But God told the Apostle to accept the food set before him.

The message of the vision was to show Peter that Christ is for all people, even those who were 'different' to him. For God makes all things 'clean' and all people 'right with Himself' through everything Jesus has done.

> *From Acts 10:11-16 (NLV)*
> *Peter saw heaven open up and something like a large linen cloth being let down to earth by the four corners. On the cloth were all kinds of four-footed animals and snakes of the earth and birds of the sky. A voice came to him, "Get up, Peter, and eat." Peter said, "No, Lord! I have never eaten anything that our Law says is unclean." The voice said the second time, "What God has made clean you must not say is unclean." This happened three times. Then it was taken back to heaven.*

While Peter was still thinking about the vision he saw, The Holy Spirit said to him that three men had arrived at the house and that God wanted him to welcome them. He also told the Apostle to go back with them, to meet Cornelius.

> *Taken from Acts 10:23-28 (The Message)*
> *The next morning Peter got up and went with them...A day later they entered Caesarea...where Cornelius and his relatives and close friends were waiting ......*

> *Cornelius went down on his face to worship Peter but Peter pulled him up and said, "None of that—I'm a man and only a man, no different from you." ...*
> *Cornelius introduced Peter to everyone who had come. Peter said, "You know, I'm sure that this is highly irregular. Jews just don't do this—visit and relax with people of another race. But God has just shown me that no race is better than any other. So I came, no questions asked".*

Cornelius explained to Peter about his angelic vision. Peter replied how he now realised that God does not show favouritism but accepts people from every nation (see Acts 10:34-35).

Peter went on to tell all who gathered there about The Good News of Jesus, and how everyone who believes in Him has their sins forgiven.

As Peter spoke, The Holy Spirit poured Himself out on the listeners. So Peter called for them all to be baptised in The Name of Jesus, and stayed with them for a few more days.

Peter returns to Jerusalem

Believers around the country heard about Peter's visit, and how Gentiles (non-Jews) received the Good News and the blessing of The Holy Spirit. Some religious (law-thinking) believers began to criticise Peter's actions.

So, when he returned to Jerusalem, Peter told the other Apostles and believers about the recent chain of events, including the visions and words God spoke. Upon hearing these things, they began to praise God and no more criticism remained.

The Church in Antioch

The news of God's Love for the Gentiles spread to Jewish believers who had previously been scattered (by persecution) to other locations.

For example, in Antioch, the church was generally spreading the Good News to fellow Jews who lived there. But after news of the events in Joppa, believers began speaking to the Greeks (Gentiles) too.

Barnabus was sent to Antioch and saw the Grace of God moving among all the people. Barnabus encouraged them and many more turned to The Lord, both Jew and Gentile.

Barnabus also travelled to Tarsus to find Saul, and brought him back to Antioch. Then both of these men stayed there for a year, teaching many people about God, and His Love and Grace towards all.

It was at Antioch that the believers first began to be known as 'Christians'.

During this time, some prophets were sent to Antioch from Jerusalem. One of these prophets, named Agabus, stood up and spoke by The Holy Spirit's leading, saying that he could foresee a famine that would spread across the land.

So, the Christians (as each one was able to) sent gifts to help those living in Judea. Saul and Barnabas took their gifts to the elders for distribution to the places where there was need.

Timeline note: The famine that Agabus 'saw prophetically' happened during the time when Claudius was emperor, and spread across the Roman world.

Peter is miraculously freed from prison

In Acts chapter 12, we see that around this time, King Herod began to arrest some of the Christians. Herod's men killed the Apostle James, and then proceeded to arrest Peter too.

Herod imprisoned Peter during the Jewish Festival of Unleavened Bread. He intended to bring Peter out of prison after The Passover, and then put him on public trial.

Peter was kept under guard by a large number of soldiers, but the church earnestly prayed for him.

The night before Herod intended to put Peter on trial, Peter was sleeping between two soldiers, bound by two chains, with sentries also guarding the entrance.

Suddenly an angel appeared in the prison cell, and a Great Light shone all around. The angel woke up Peter and told him to get up. As he did so, the chains fell off his wrists.

The angel then instructed Peter to get dressed and to follow him out of the prison. Peter thought he was seeing a vision, and did not really understand what was happening as they passed by the guards.

When Peter and the angel came to the city gates, the gates opened for them as though 'by themselves'. After walking through one of the streets, the angel left Peter. Then Peter realise what was happening and that God had rescued him!

So, he continued walking to the house where Mary lived.

Many people had gathered at Mary's house to pray, so when Peter knocked on the door, a servant named Rhoda came to ask who was there.

When she recognised Peter's voice she ran back to tell all the others in the house, but forgot to open the door in her excitement! At first no one believed her.

Peter kept knocking, so when they finally opened the door everyone was astonished to see him there in person. He explained to his brothers and sisters all that had happened, and then after the brief reunion, he left to go to another place for safety.

When morning came, the soldiers were baffled and there was a commotion about where Peter had gone. A furious Herod ordered a search and cross-examined the guards.

When Herod travelled from Judea to Caesarea, he met with the people of Tyre and Sidon, who he had a conflict with. But they asked to see him to seek peace because they depended on him for food.

So, when he came out to speak to the crowds, dressed in his royal robes, the people began to shout, "this is the voice of a god, not a man". But as they did so, Herod died suddenly.

> *Acts 12:24-25 (The Message)*
> *Meanwhile, the ministry of God's Word grew by leaps and bounds. Barnabas and Saul, once they had delivered the relief offering to the church in Jerusalem, went back to Antioch. This time they took John with them, the one they called Mark.*

THE GOOD NEWS OF CHRIST IS FOR EVERY TRIBE, TONGUE AND NATION

A SIMPLE LOOK AT ACTS CHAPTERS 13-28

Acts 1:8
Jesus told His Disciples: you will receive power when the Holy Spirit comes upon you. And you will be My witnesses, telling people about Me everywhere—in Jerusalem, throughout Judea, in Samaria, and TO THE ENDS OF THE EARTH."

A SIMPLE OVERVIEW OF ACTS CHAPTERS 13-28

Barnabus and Saul (also called Paul) are sent out

In Acts Chapter 13, we see how The Holy Spirit spoke to the prophets and teachers of the church in Antioch, instructing them to set apart Barnabas and Saul to travel. After praying for the men, the church sent them out in the power of God's Spirit to speak about Jesus near and far.

Barnabas and Saul sailed to the Island of Cyprus, where they spoke the message of God to the synagogues, across the whole island. John Mark was with them to help.

At the city of Paphos, they met a man named Elymas (also known as Barjesus) who practised magic but was a false prophet. When the Governor invited Barnabus and Saul to share God's message with him, Elymas spoke against them. Elymas was trying to prevent the Governor believing in Jesus.

But Saul (also known as Paul) was empowered by The Holy Spirit and prophesied into the situation. For a while Elymas could not see and could no longer interfere, so the Governor was able to hear the message and believed.

Paul and his companions continued to travel to speak to the people, but John Mark went back to Jerusalem. When Paul spoke again in one of the synagogues, he told the people about the history that led to the coming of Christ and all God had done for them.

Many people wanted to hear more, but some jealousy developed in the community of the attention the men received. Some religious people became angry and drove the Apostles out of the town. But those who believed continued to rejoice in the message Paul had brought.

Barnabus and Paul continue to travel and teach

In Acts Chapter 14, we see Paul and Barnabus traveling to Iconium ~ a city that was in ancient 'Asia Minor' (modern day 'Turkey').

As they taught about Jesus, many Jews and Greeks believed. The Apostles stayed in the city for some time and continued to speak with boldness. The men taught the people about the Grace and Mercy of God, and miraculous signs followed the teaching of His Word.

However, the city became divided in what people chose to believe. When Paul and Barnabus heard that some people had become angry and were making plans to harm them, they moved on.

The Apostles travelled to the cities in Lycaonia (a region inside Asia Minor). In the city of Lystra, there was a man who had never been able to walk. The man was sat listening to Paul sharing about Jesus, when Paul had a word of knowledge that this man had faith in God to heal him.

Empowered by The Holy Spirit, Paul looked at the man and shouted, "stand to your feet"; the man immediately jumped up and began walking. When the people saw what happened, they thought Paul and Barnabus must be 'gods' and began to call Barnabus 'Zeus' and Paul 'Hermes'.

A priest from the temple of Zeus (nearby) brought bulls and flowers to the city gate, where he and a crowd of people wanted to offer a sacrifice to Paul and Barnabus. But The Apostles tried to stop them, telling the people 'we are not gods, we are men just like you'.

> *Acts 14:14-18 (NIV)*
> *When the apostles Barnabas and Paul heard of this, they tore their clothes* (a sign of distress) *and rushed out into the crowd, shouting: "Friends, why are you doing this? We too are only human, like you. We are bringing you good news, telling you to turn from these worthless things to the living God, who made the heavens and the earth and the sea and everything in them. In the past, he let all nations go their own way. Yet he has not left himself without testimony: He has shown kindness by giving you rain from heaven and crops in their seasons; he provides you with plenty of food and fills your hearts with joy." Even with these words, they had difficulty keeping the crowd from sacrificing to them.*

Some of the people threw stones at Paul and dragged him out of the town, leaving him there for dead. But the followers of Christ gathered around Paul's body and ministered to him. Miraculously, he got up and walked back into the town.

The following day Paul and Barnabus travelled on to the city of Derbe, where many people gave their hearts to Jesus.

After this, The Apostles returned to the cities of Lystra, Iconium and Antioch to encourage the believers there. Paul and Barnabus spent some time there, chose Elders for each church and prayed for them.

Paul and Barnabus then travelled through many more areas of Asia Minor and preached in a number of cities, before finally sailing back to Antioch in Syria.

The Apostles gave their amazing testimonies to the church that had sent them out, and told them about everything God had done for both Jews and Gentiles (non-Jews) alike.

In their travels, Paul and Barnabus saw that God showed His Love and Grace to everyone, whoever they were and wherever they were, as they shared the message of Jesus.

The Meeting at Jerusalem

Also referred to as the meeting of 'THE JERUSALEM COUNCIL'

In Acts Chapter 15, we read about Paul and Barnabus arguing with some men, who had come from Judea. These men had begun to teach non-Jewish believers that they had to be circumcised. [Circumcision of the first born male was required in 'The Law of Moses', which was a set of rules that the Jewish religion observed].

So, Paul, Barnabus and some others from the church were sent to Jerusalem to talk with the rest of The Apostles and The Elders of The Church about this subject in more depth. As they travelled, they encouraged believers in each country they went through.

At Jerusalem, the church gathered to welcome them and praised God for all He had done. However, some believers began to repeat that Gentile believers must be instructed to obey The Law of Moses. After a long study and debate, Peter stood up and spoke to the meeting.

Peter shared how God was saving Jews and Gentiles in the same manner, by His Grace, when anyone put faith in Christ. He said that God had always planned to do this.

Acts 15:7-11 (NIV)
After much discussion, Peter got up and addressed them: "Brothers, you know that some time ago God made a choice among you that the Gentiles might hear from my lips the message of the gospel and believe. God, who knows the heart, showed that he accepted them by giving the Holy Spirit to them, just as he did to us.
He did not discriminate between us and them, for he purified their hearts by faith. Now then, why do you try to test God by putting on the necks of Gentiles a yoke that neither we nor our ancestors have been able to bear? No! We believe it is through the grace of our Lord Jesus that we are saved, just as they are."

After Peter had spoken, the gathering became quiet. Paul and Barnabus told them all about the miracles God had performed for both Jews and Gentiles, freely by His Grace. Then James spoke and suggested that a letter be sent to Gentiles believers to report the conclusion of the meeting.

From Acts 15:22-31 (The Message)
Everyone agreed: apostles, leaders, all the people. They picked Judas (nicknamed Barsabbas) and Silas.....and sent them to Antioch with Paul and Barnabas with this letter:

From the apostles and leaders, your friends, to our friends in Antioch, Syria, and Cilicia: We heard that some men from our church went to you and said things that confused you....we didn't send them. We have agreed unanimously to pick representatives and send them to you with our good friends Barnabas and Paul. We picked men we knew you could trust, Judas and Silas....

> *...We've sent them to confirm in a face-to-face meeting with you what we've written. It seemed to the Holy Spirit and to us that you should not be saddled with any crushing burden, but be responsible only for these bare necessities: Be careful not to get involved in activities connected with idols; avoid serving food offensive to Jewish Christians (blood, for instance); and guard the morality of sex and marriage. These guidelines are sufficient to keep relations congenial between us. And God be with you!*

When the men (along with Paul and Barnabus) went to Antioch with the letter, the believers gratefully received the report.

Paul and Barnabus separate

After a short while at Antioch, Paul and Barnabas decided to go back to all the towns where they had preached to see how the believers were getting on.

Barnabas wanted to take John Mark with them but Paul did not think that was wise (because John Mark had left them during a previous trip, at a time of trouble).

Paul and Barnabus disagreed on this issue to such an extent that, they chose to go separate ways. Barnabas sailed to Cyprus with John Mark and Paul set out with Silas to the countries of Syria and Cilicia.

Timothy joins Paul and Silas

In Acts Chapter 16, we see Paul in the city of Derbe, where there was a believer named Timothy (whose mother was a Jewish believer and whose father was Greek). Paul wanted Timothy to travel with him.

So, to avoid a potential conflict with some of the people he would meet along the way, Paul decided to circumcise Timothy. Paul and his team, including Timothy, then went through various cities to encourage the believers, and gave them the information from the Meeting at Jerusalem. The churches became stronger in their faith, and the number of believers grew each day.

Paul called to Macedonia

During their traveling, Paul had a vision where he saw a man from Macedonia stand before him, pleading with him to come to Macedonia and help the people there. Paul immediately prepared to leave for Macedonia, recognizing that God had called him to speak the Good News there too.

The team sailed to the island of Samothrace and to the city of Neapolis. They went on to travel to Philippi (a Roman colony) which was the leading city in that part of Macedonia. While they were there, the team came across a group of women and began a conversation with them.

A woman named Lydia (from the city of Thyatira) was one of these women. She was known in the city as a seller of purple cloth. Lydia listened to Paul and put her faith in Jesus; so she and her whole household were baptised. Paul and his team then stayed for a while with her household to encourage them.

Paul and Silas are put in jail

In the marketplace of the city, there was a servant girl who had an unclean spirit (that is, not of God) through which she practised fortune telling.

The girl's owners earned a lot of money using her to manipulate people with her 'gift'. She began to follow Paul and his team shouting (and mocking) saying, "These men are servants of the Most-High God! They are telling you how you can be saved!"

After several days, Paul turned around and said to the spirit, "By the power of Jesus Christ, I command you to come out of her!" Immediately, the unclean spirit left.

When the men who owned the servant girl saw that they could no longer use her to make money, they grabbed Paul and Silas, and dragged them into the public square to stand before the Roman officials. The owners of the girl said to everyone, "These men are making trouble in our city"

The crowd turned against Paul and Silas, and the officials ordered that they be beaten with rods and thrown into jail. The officials told the jailer to guard them very carefully. So the jailer put Paul and Silas deep inside the jail and bound their feet between large blocks of wood.

Earthquake at Midnight

Around midnight, Paul and Silas were praying and singing songs to God, while the other prisoners were listening. Suddenly there was an earthquake which shook the foundation of the jail. All the doors of the jail opened, and the chains on all of the prisoners fell off. The jailer woke up and saw doors open, and was terrified.

He assumed the prisoners had escaped, so he got his sword and was ready to kill himself (because he was frightened of the consequences from The Roman Authorities). But Paul shouted, "Don't hurt yourself! We are all here!"

The jailer came and saw that everyone was there, so he fell down in front of Paul and Silas asking them what he needed to do to be saved. They replied, "Believe in the Lord Jesus and you will be saved—you and your household."

Paul and Silas shared God's Love and Grace with the jailer and all who lived with him. The jailer washed the prisoners wounds, and then his whole household were baptised. He also ensured that Paul and Silas had plenty food and water.

The next morning the officials sent soldiers to tell the jailer, "Let these men go free." The jailer said to Paul, "You can leave now. Go in peace."

But Paul said to the soldiers, "The officials did not prove that we did anything wrong, but they beat us in public and put us in jail, but we are Roman citizens. Now they want us to go away quietly. No, they must come here themselves and lead us out!" So the soldiers went back to the officials.

When the officials heard that Paul and Silas were Roman citizens they were afraid; because it was against the law to beat a Roman citizen before a trial. So they went to apologise. The officials led Paul and Silas out of the jail and asked them to leave the city. They went to Lydia's house to encourage the believers, and then they left the city.

Paul and Silas in Thessalonica

In Acts Chapter 17, we see that Paul and Silas then travelled through the cities of Amphipolis and Apollonia. When they arrived at the city of Thessalonica, Paul went to the synagogue. For three weeks, on each Sabbath day, he examined the Scriptures with them.

Paul explained how the Scriptures showed that The Messiah (Jesus) had to die and then rise from the dead, to save all people in the whole world. Many believed Paul and Silas, and joined them, along with a large number of Gentiles and women.

However, a crowd formed in the city and a riot began. The mob went to Jason's house, looking for Paul and Silas. When they did not find them, they dragged Jason and some of the other believers to stand before the city leaders.

The crowd shouted that the men had caused trouble and Jason was keeping them in his house. The mob claimed the men had broken the 'law of Caesar' by preaching that Jesus is King. The city leaders fined Jason and the believers, then ordered them not to cause any further trouble.

Paul and Silas go to Berea

After the events at Thessalonica, Paul and Silas travelled on to a city named Berea. Paul went to the synagogue and taught the people there. They studied the Scriptures to check what he said, and thus received the message joyfully.

When some people who had objected to Paul's teaching back in Thessalonica heard that he was teaching in Berea, they came to cause trouble. So, Paul went on to the coast, while Silas and Timothy remained in Berea.

Paul in Athens

(Paul's speech at 'Mars Hill')

Paul travelled on to Athens and sent a message back to Silas and Timothy (still in Berea) to come and join him as soon as possible.

In Athens, Paul was troubled that the city was full of idols. So he preached at the synagogue and also went into the public square to share the message of Christ. The people of Athens spent much of their time debating all the latest ideas, so some philosophers came to discuss with Paul this 'new idea' that he was preaching. The place they spoke at was known as 'Mars Hill'.

As Paul spoke, he pointed to the people's worship of different 'gods' and drew their attention to the altar that they had made, dedicated to the 'unknown god' (Paul used something the people could relate to, in order to help them understand his message). Then Paul explained:

> 'It is The One True God that people need to know. For God created everything in heaven and earth, and He sent Jesus to pay for all sin, for everyone, across all time. God made all the different people who live everywhere in the world'. 'In the past people did not understand Him, but He overlooked this. Now, He is calling people everywhere to know Him as He truly is, through Christ whom God raised from the dead'.

Some of the listeners laughed at Paul but others believed. Among those who joined Paul was a man called Dionysius and a woman named Damaris.

Paul in Corinth

In Acts Chapter 18, we see Paul leave Athens and go to the city of Corinth. There he met a man named Aquila and his wife Priscilla, who were tentmakers like himself. Paul stayed with Aquilla and Priscilla, and continued to talk to people about Jesus wherever he went.

When some religious people in the city disagreed sharply with Paul, he responded by shaking the dust from his feet (a symbolic sign that he was moving on).

But God spoke to Paul in a vision saying, 'Do not be afraid; do not stop sharing My Message. For I AM with you, and you will not come to harm. Many of My People are in this city." So Paul went to the home of Titius Justus, stayed for a year and a half teaching people, and baptising believers.

During this time, a man named Gallio was the Governor of Achaia. Some people came together against Paul and took him to court. They complained to Gallio that Paul was teaching people to worship God in a way that was against their religious practice. But Gallio replied that he would only listen if the complaint were about a crime, then he made them leave the court.

Paul returns to Antioch (via Ephesus)

When Paul decided to travel back to Antioch, he took Priscilla and Aquila with him. At a place called Cenchrea Paul cut off his hair, which was an outward sign that Paul used to show he had fulfilled a vow he had made to God.

Paul then travelled to Ephesus with Priscilla and Aquila. Once they were there, they said goodbye to Paul. While Paul was visiting Ephesus, he spoke at the synagogue as was his custom. The people wanted him to stay, so he said he would come back if God led him that way again.

Paul travelled to Caesarea and Jerusalem on his way to Antioch. After staying in Antioch for a while, Paul went through Galatia and Phrygia, teaching and helping the believers there.

Apollos in Ephesus and Corinth

A man named Apollos came to Ephesus, who was eager to teach people about Jesus. Apollos was born in the city of Alexandria and had been taught about The Lord, but the only baptism he knew was that of John the Baptist.

When Priscilla and Aquila heard Apollos speak boldly in the synagogue, they invited him to their home and helped him understand more about the baptism of The Holy Spirit (being filled with God's Spirit).

Apollos wanted to go to Achaia (an area lying on the southern shore of The Corinthian Gulf). So, the believers in Ephesus wrote a letter to the believers at Achaia, asking them to welcome Apollos. When he arrived there, he helped people know more about God's Grace and used the Scriptures to show that Jesus truly was (is) the Messiah.

Paul in Ephesus

In Acts Chapter 19, we see Paul travelling back to Ephesus again. In the city, Paul also found some believers who had not heard of being filled with The Holy Spirit. So, he began to teach them that John The Baptist showed the way to repentance and baptised people in water as an outward sign of trusting in Christ.

Paul explained how The Holy Spirit empowers believers to live in the way God intends, as people listen to Him. The believers were then baptised in water and filled with The Holy Spirit as Paul placed his hands on them. As the believers were filled, they began speaking in different languages and prophesying.

Over the next three months, Paul spoke boldly at the synagogue. Many accepted his message while some did not. Those who rejected Paul began to speak accusations about The Way (the name given to the followers of Christ).

> *John 14:6 (NLV)*
> *Jesus said, "I am the Way and the Truth and the Life. No one can go to the Father except by Me*

So, Paul and the believers went to a place where a man named Tyrannus had a school, and there Paul talked with people daily. Through Paul's teaching over the next two years, everyone in Asia heard the Good News.

More healings and miracles

God performed extraordinary miracles through Paul. For example: some people took handkerchiefs and clothes that Paul had used and placed them on those who were sick or oppressed. When they did this, the sick were healed and any oppressive or tormenting spirits left people.

The Sons of Sceva

At that time, there was a group of men (the seven sons of a man named Sceva) that tried to make demons come out of people. This group (who were not believers) tried to force evil spirits to obey them. The result of their effort can be seen in the verses below:

> *From Acts 19:14-20 (GNT)*
> *When the sons Sceva were doing this... the evil spirit said to them, "I know Jesus, and I know about Paul; but you—who are you?" The man who had the evil spirit in him attacked them (the sons Sceva) with such violence that he overpowered them all.*

They ran away from his house, wounded and with their clothes torn off. All the Jews and Gentiles who lived in Ephesus heard about this; they were all filled with fear, and the name of the Lord Jesus was given greater honor. Many of the believers came, publicly admitting and revealing what they had done. Many of those who had practiced magic brought their books together and burned them in public. They added up the price of the books, and the total came to fifty thousand silver coins. In this powerful way the word of the Lord kept spreading and growing stronger.

Paul makes plans for his next journey

After these events, Paul began to make plans to travel to Macedonia and Achaia, and then to go on to Jerusalem. He also wanted to visit Rome; but he stayed in Asia for a while longer. So, Paul sent Timothy and Erastus ahead of him to Macedonia, to prepare the way.

Riot in Ephesus

Meanwhile, trouble was being stirred up in Ephesus. Some men who were skilled in working with silver ~ who could make many different things with their ability ~ became angry by change happening in the city.

One of the things that the silver-workers made were silver models that looked like the temple of the goddess Artemis. The men made a great deal of money from selling these models as 'idols'.

But since Paul and his companions had preached in the city, many people had turned away from worshiping false gods, and less of the models were being sold.

One of the silver workers, a man named Demetrius, called his fellow workers together to discuss their problem. The men decided to stir up the people to go back to worshipping the 'gods' they used to, so that the men could sell their models. The men went into the city and shouted, 'Artemis is the goddess that everyone in Asia and the whole world worships. Great is Artemis, the goddess of Ephesus!'

Chaos and confusion developed among the people. A crowd grabbed Gaius and Aristarchus (companions of Paul) and dragged them into a stadium. Paul wanted to go and talk with the people but the believers told him to hold back. There was great arguing and disorder in the stadium, so a man named Alexander stood up and tried to bring calm.

However, the commotion continued and the crowd shouted for the next two hours: "Great is Artemis of Ephesus!" Finally, the City Clerk came and managed to persuade the crowd to calm down. He told them that Ephesus would be keeping the Temple of Artemis, and told the people that Paul's companions had not spoken against their religion.

The Clerk also told the silver-workers that they must attend the council meetings in the city to discuss complaints, and then he dispersed the crowd.

Paul goes to Macedonia and Greece

In Acts Chapter 20, we see Paul encouraging the believers in Ephesus, after the trouble, and then he moved on to travel through Macedonia. He spoke to numerus people on his journey, encouraging them in the Love of God. When he arrived in Greece, he stayed for three months.

Paul wanted to sail to Syria, but found out that some people were making a plot against him; so he chose to go back through Macedonia to reach Syria.

Some of Paul's companions went ahead of him: Sopater, Aristarchus, Secundus, Gaius, Timothy, Tychicus and Trophimus. These men waited for Paul in the city of Troas. After the Festival of Unleavened Bread, Paul and Luke set sail from the city of Philippi and met the rest of their companions in Troas five days later.

A young man is raised from the dead

Paul shared The Lord's Supper with a group of believers the day before he was planning to travel on again. He talked with the group until midnight in an upper room. A young man named Eutychus was sitting in the window listening to Paul, and as he continued talking, Eutychus became drowsy.

After a while, the young man went to sleep and fell out of the window. Having fallen from the third floor to the ground below, Eutychus died. Paul immediately went down and knelt next to him, held the young man in his arms, and said to the other believers, "Don't worry, he is alive now."

Then Paul went back upstairs, ate some bread, and continued to speak throughout the night! In the morning, after finishing his talk, Paul left to continue his travels. The people joyfully took Eutychus home, alive and well.

Paul travels again, by land and sea

Paul's companions set sail with the plan to meet him at the city of Assos (Paul wanted to travel there by land).

When Paul caught up with his friends at Assos, they took him on board, and sailed on to Mitylene. From there they sailed towards the island of Chios and the island of Samos, and arrived at the city of Miletus a day later. Paul decided not to stop at Ephesus on this occasion, because he wanted to reach Jerusalem in time for the Festival of Pentecost.

Paul speaks to The Elders from Ephesus

At Miletus, Paul sent a message to The Elders of the church in Ephesus asking them to come and meet with him. When they came, Paul reassured them that he cared for the church at Ephesus but explained that he must now go on to Jerusalem. Paul also told them that this would be the last time he saw them and gave them instructions on how to look after the church when he had gone. After talking and praying together, they said goodbye to Paul, with sadness, as he set sail again for Jerusalem.

Paul travels to Jerusalem

In Acts Chapter 21 we see Paul and his companions set sail to Syria. The ship travelled pass many islands on its way, and stopped at Tyre because it needed to unload its cargo there.

Paul and his friends found the believers in Tyre, and stayed with them for seven days. The believers warned Paul not to go to Jerusalem but when the ship was ready again, Paul continued his journey.

From Tyre, they went to the city of Ptolemais, and stayed with the believers there for a day. After this, Paul went to the city of Caesarea, and stayed at the home of Philip and his daughters (who had the gift of prophesy).

Some days later, a man named Agabus came to see Paul and prophesied to him:

> *From Acts 21:10-14 (TLB)*
> *During our stay of several days, a man named Agabus, who also had the gift of prophecy, arrived from Judea and visited us... He took Paul's belt, bound his own feet and hands with it, and said, "The Holy Spirit declares, 'So shall the owner of this belt be bound...in Jerusalem and turned over to the Romans'" ...*
>
> *Hearing this, the local believers and his traveling companions begged Paul not to go on to Jerusalem. But he said, "Why all this weeping? ...For I am ready not only to be jailed at Jerusalem but also to die for the sake of the Lord Jesus."*

So, Paul and his friends (and some believers from Caesarea) began to get ready for the next part of their journey. After staying at the home of Mnason, a man from Cyprus, they all set off together for Jerusalem.

Paul visits James

When Paul reached Jerusalem, he was greeted warmly by the believers. He went to visit James (along with his companions) and all The Elders there.

Paul spoke to them about the wonderful things God had done during his travels, among both Jews and Gentiles alike.

At The Elders request, Paul accompanied four men to The Temple, to share in their religious cleansing ceremony. After the ceremony, Paul announced that the need for religious rituals was coming to an end.

Paul is arrested

Some people who saw Paul in The Temple area began to stir up trouble among those gathered there. They misinformed people about Paul and his intentions, triggering an angry reaction in the city.

A crowd grabbed Paul and dragged him away from the 'holy area' and sought to kill him. When The Commander of The Roman Army in Jerusalem heard about the riot, he immediately went with his soldiers to disperse the crowd.

He stopped the beating of Paul but arrested him and told the soldiers to tie him up with two chains. The Commander tried to find out who Paul was and what the riot was about, but they was a great deal of confusion and shouting from the people gathered around.

As Paul was taken to the army building, a mob followed behind, so the soldiers carried Paul up the steps to protect him. Paul then turned to speak to The Commander, to explain who he was and where his was from. He asked to be able to speak to the crowd, and The Commander agreed.

Paul speaks to the people

In Acts Chapter 22 Paul begins to speak to the crowd in their own language:

> *From Acts 22:1-21 (NCV)*
> *Paul said, "...listen to my defence...." When they heard him speaking their language, they became very quiet. Paul said, "I am a Jew, born in Tarsus in the country of Cilicia, but I grew up in this city. I was a student of Gamaliel, who carefully taught me everything about the law of our ancestors.*

I was very serious about serving God, just as are all of you here today. I persecuted the people who followed The Way of Jesus, and some of them were even killed. I arrested men and women and put them in jail. The high priest and the whole council of elders can tell you this is true. They gave me letters to the brothers in Damascus.

So I was going there to arrest these people and bring them back to Jerusalem to be punished. "About noon when I came near Damascus, a bright light from heaven suddenly flashed all around me. I fell to the ground and heard a voice saying, 'Saul, Saul, why are you persecuting me?'
I asked, 'Who are you, Lord?' The voice said, 'I am Jesus from Nazareth whom you are persecuting.' Those who were with me did not understand the voice, but they saw the light. I said, 'What shall I do, Lord?'

The Lord answered, 'Get up and go to Damascus. There you will be told about all the things I have planned for you to do.' I could not see, because the bright light had made me blind. So my companions led me into Damascus. "There a man named Ananias came to me. He was a religious man; he obeyed the law of Moses, and all the Jews who lived there respected him. He stood by me and said, 'Brother Saul, see again!' Immediately I was able to see him.

He said, 'The God of our ancestors chose you long ago to know his plan, to see the Righteous One, and to hear words from him. You will be his witness to all people, telling them about what you have seen and heard... Get up, be baptized, and wash your sins away, trusting in him to save you.'

"Later, when I returned to Jerusalem, I was praying in the Temple, and I saw a vision. I saw the Lord saying to me... 'Leave now. I will send you far away to the other nations.'"

The crowd listened for a while, but then began to threaten Paul again. So he was taken inside the building. While the soldiers were beating Paul, he said to the Army Officer: "Do you have the right to beat a Roman citizen who has not been proven guilty?"

On hearing this, The Officer he went to The Commander to report that Paul was a Roman citizen. The Commander became afraid, as it was not lawful to beat a Roman Citizen that had not been found guilty of a crime. The following day, The Commander ordered that Paul's chains were removed and called on the religious council to meet and discuss the situation.

Charges against Paul

In Acts Chapter 24, we see the meeting take place, where religious leaders bring a lawyer with them named Tertullus. The leaders went to Caesarea to bring their charges against Paul, so that the case could be brought before The Governor of Judea, a man named Felix. Paul was summoned to the meeting, as Tertullus addressed Felix to make their accusations:

> *From Acts 24:3-8*
> *Your Excellency, we are very grateful to you. But I don't want to bore you, so please give me your attention for only a moment. We have found this man to be a troublemaker who is constantly stirring up riots all over the world. He is a ringleader of the cult known as the Nazarenes. Furthermore, he was trying to desecrate the Temple when we arrested him. You can find out the truth of our accusations by examining him yourself."*

Paul defends himself before Felix

When Felix beckoned Paul to speak, he then gave his own testimony and defence:

> *From Acts 24:10-21(The Message)*
> *Paul said, "I count myself fortunate to be defending myself before you, Governor, knowing how fair-minded you've been in judging us all these years. I've been back in the country only twelve days... I came with the express purpose of worshiping in Jerusalem on Pentecost, and I've been minding my own business the whole time. Nobody can say they saw me arguing in the Temple or working up a crowd in the streets. Not one of their charges can be backed up with evidence or witnesses.*
>
> *"But I do freely admit this: In regard to the Way...I serve and worship the very same God served and worshiped by all our ancestors and embrace everything written in all our Scriptures. And I admit to living in hopeful anticipation that God will raise the dead, both the good and the bad....*
>
> *I do my level best to keep a clear conscience before God and my neighbours in everything I do. I've been out of the country for a number of years and now I'm back. While I was away, I took up a collection for the poor and brought that with me, along with offerings for the Temple.*
>
> *It was while making those offerings that they found me quietly at my prayers in the Temple....It's because I believe in the resurrection that I've been hauled into this court! Does that sound to you like grounds for a criminal case?"*

Felix knew quite a lot about 'The Way', so he stopped the trial and said that he would decide what to do when Commander Lysias arrived.

Felix told the Army Officer to guard Paul but to let his companions bring whatever he needed.

Paul speaks to Felix and his wife

A few days later, Felix asked for Paul to be sent to speak to him and his wife Drusilla. Paul spoke to them about believing in Christ, which they listened to. But Felix became afraid when Paul spoke about the need of self-control, and to make right choices and judgments. At this point Felix dismissed Paul.

Felix had hoped Paul would pay him a bribe at some point, but despite the many visits Paul would not do this. So Felix left Paul in prison. After two years, Porcius Festus replaced Felix as Governor.

Paul asks to see Caesar

In Acts Chapter 25 we see the religious leaders bringing their charges against Paul before the new Governor Festus. While he was in Jerusalem, Paul's accusers asked Festus to send Paul back to their city (because they secretly planned to kill him on his way there).

But Festus refused their request, and said that Paul would stay in Caesarea. When the Governor was back in Caesarea, he called the soldiers to bring Paul before him. Festus sat on the Judgment Seat while the leaders brought their charges against Paul, but they could not prove any of them.

Festus asked Paul if he wanted to go to Jerusalem to be judged there, but Paul replied, "I want Caesar to hear my case!" After talking with his advisers, Festus agreed to send Paul to Caesar.

A few days later King Agrippa and Bernice came to visit Festus, so he told the king about Paul's case. Agrippa said that he would like to hear Paul. Thus, another meeting was arranged for the King to question Paul and hear both sides of the argument for himself.

Paul stands before King Agrippa

In Acts Chapter 26, we see the meeting taking place (following a grand entrance by King Agrippa, full of pomp and ceremony). After receiving his fill of attention, Agrippa then turned to Paul to tell him to speak. Paul told the king his testimony and defence in the same way that he had previously spoken to Felix.

While Paul was still speaking, Festus shouted at him accusing him of being out of his mind. Paul replied that he was not crazy but that everything he said was true. Paul then turned to Agrippa and asked him if he believed the Prophets of The Old Testament.

The king responded by asking Paul if he thought he could so easily persuade him to become a 'Christ-follower'. Then Paul prayed that everyone listening would be saved, like him but without the chains. At this everyone left the room. After this, they decided to send Paul to Caesar as he had previously requested.

Paul sails for Rome

In Acts Chapter 27, we see Paul set sail for Italy, with an Army Officer named Julius put in charge of him. The ship had other prisoners on board as well as Paul, as it travelled the long voyage.

The journey was not a smooth one, and the navigation of the ship had to be changed several times. When the sailing became dangerous, Paul warned those around him that he foresaw serious trouble ahead, but The Captain and The Owner of the ship disagreed.

While they were sailing close to the island of Crete, a mighty wind caught the sails of the ship. When this happened, the ship could only travel in the same direction as the wind was blowing.

The sailors tried to anchor the ship many times, but to no avail. When the storm became overpowering, they began to throw things out of the boat, including equipment that helped them navigate by the stars.

After several days, the men began to lose hope and they thought they would all die. They stopped eating for some time. Then one day Paul stood and said to them all that he had seen an angel in a vision who spoke to him from God. Paul told the men:

> *From Acts 27:23-26*
> *...last night an angel of God .. stood beside me, and he said, 'Don't be afraid, Paul, for you will surely stand trial before Caesar! God in his goodness has granted safety to everyone sailing with you.' So take courage! I believe God...But we will be shipwrecked on an island."*

One night, while the ship was still being blown around by the storm, the sailors believed they were close to land so thcy threw a rope into the water to test the depth. When they thought they were getting closer to land, they threw four anchors into the water, and waited for daylight.

However, in a state of confusion, and with a fear of hitting rocks, some of the sailors wanted to leave the ship. So, those who wanted to leave lowered the lifeboat into the water. Paul spoke to the Army Officer and the soldiers, saying that this fearful action could cost everyone their lives. So the soldiers cut the ropes and let the lifeboat fall into the water.

Just before dawn, Paul managed to encourage everyone to eat something. At daylight, the sailors saw land (but they did not know where they were). They saw a bay, with a beach and tried to sail the ship as close to the beach as possible. But the ship hit a sandbank and the front of the vessel could not move.

Then the large waves of the sea began to break the back of the ship to pieces. The soldiers wanted to kill the prisoners so that none of them could swim away and escape. But Julius wanted to let Paul live, so he did not allow the soldiers to kill anyone. Instead, the Army Officer told everyone to swim or use pieces of the ship to help them get safely to land.

Paul reaches Malta

In Acts Chapter 28, we see that the island they had all landed on was Malta. The people who lived there welcomed the shipwrecked men, and helped them to build a fire to keep them warm (since it was raining and very cold).

While Paul was putting more sticks on the pile of wood that they had lit to make a fire, a poisonous snake came out from under the pile (because of the heat) and bit Paul's hand.

Paul shook off the snake, sending it back into the fire and stood unhurt. The people were astonished, as they expected him to die from the snake's poison. But he continued as if nothing had happened and suffered no ill effects from the venom.

A man on the island welcomed the new visitors into his home. His name was Publius, and he was the most important Roman official there. Paul prayed for the man's father who was sick, laid hands on him, and he recovered. After this, all the sick people on the island came to Paul, and he healed them too.

After about three months, the kindness and generosity of the island's people provided everything the men needed to set sail again. So, Paul (still under guard) boarded a ship which had been anchored at Malta during the winter.

After stopping at a number of places on route, Paul finally reached Rome. When believers in the city heard that he was there, they came out to greet him. Paul thanked God and was encouraged by them.

Paul in Rome

At Rome, Paul was allowed to live alone but a soldier stayed with him to continue guarding him. Paul sent for some key religious leaders to talk with them about the disagreements that had taken place.

He told the leaders that he was not against anyone, he was only sharing the Good News of Jesus. Some of the leaders believed him. Paul stayed for two years in a rented house in Rome, and he welcomed all who came to visit him.

Paul told everyone about God's Eternal Kingdom and His Love for all people. Paul continued to be bold, and kept speaking the message of salvation for all through faith in God's Son.

~~~~~~~

As promised in Acts 1:8 ~ starting at Jerusalem, throughout Judea and to the ends of the earth ~ God continues to send out His Message of Reconciliation.

His Holy Spirit speaks every day through people all over the world ~ whenever they share His Love and Grace by speaking good words, and sharing acts of kindness.

In Christ, God came to man. He reconciled us to Himself through Jesus at The Cross. Through Him we can each have a personal relationship with God that lasts forever. Jesus is alive for all eternity. And we shall live with Him.

No one is rejected when they come to The Son. For God is Love, and Jesus has shown us what God is really like.

~~~~~~~

Taken from John 1:12,14,18 / John 6:38 (NIV)

....to all who believed Him (Jesus) and accepted Him, He gave the right to become children of God....

The Word (speaking of Christ) became human and made His home among us. He was full of unfailing love and faithfulness. And we have seen the glory of the Father's one and only Son.....He has revealed God to us.....

Jesus said: "whoever comes to Me I will never drive away"

Section Four

INTRODUCING
THE NEW TESTAMENT
LETTERS WHICH
OFFER INSIGHT
FOR ALL
GENERATIONS

New Testament Letters (part 1)

INTRODUCING THE NEW TESTAMENT LETTERS (Part 1)

Paul's Letters *(Also known as the 'Pauline Epistles')*

The Books are listed below as they appear in The New Testament. For chronological order please see timeline in section six.

ROMANS is a letter that was written by The Apostle Paul to the believers in Rome {which was delivered to the church by 'Phoebe' (Rom 16:1-2)} Approximate date of writing: 55-58 AD.

Purpose of writing:
To teach about the Righteousness of God; to show that everyone needs His Grace and Mercy; to explain that salvation is received by putting faith in Christ ~ who came for ALL people, everywhere.

Overall theme of chapters:

- 1-3 ~ The need for God's Righteousness
- 4-5 ~ God credits righteousness to us by faith
- 6-8 ~ The meaning of His Righteousness
- 9-11 ~ All who call on Him are saved
- 12-13 ~ Dedication to God / Respect for others
- 14-15 ~ Compassion / Spiritual Hope
- 16 ~ All are important to God

Some key verses:

Taken from Rom 1:16-17 (NCV)
I am not ashamed of the Good News, because it is the power God uses to save everyone who believes...The Good News shows how God makes people right with himself...

Taken from Rom 4:5, 5:1, 6:23, 8:1+38
People are counted as righteous because of their faith in God.... Since we have been made right in God's sight we have peace because of what Jesus has done for us....For the free gift of God is eternal life through Christ.. So now there is no condemnation for those who belong to Jesus....And because you belong to him, the power of the life-giving Spirit has freed you from the power of sin....for nothing can keep us from the love of God.

Taken from Rom 10:9-13 (NIV)
For if you declare with your mouth, "Jesus is Lord," and believe in your heart that God raised him from the dead, you will be saved. For it is with your heart that you believe and are justified, and it is with your mouth that you profess your faith and are saved.....there is no difference between Jew and Gentile—the same Lord is Lord of all and richly blesses all who call on him.

Taken from Rom 12:1-2 (The Message)
So here's what I want you to do, God helping you: Take your everyday, ordinary life—your sleeping, eating, going-to-work, and walking-around life—and place it before God as an offering. Embracing what God does for you is the best thing you can do for him. Don't become so well-adjusted to your culture that you fit into it without even thinking. Instead, fix your attention on God. You'll be changed from the inside out.

Taken from Rom 15:5-6+13 (NIV)
May the God who gives endurance and encouragement give you the same attitude of mind toward each other that Christ Jesus had, so that with one mind and one voice you may glorify the God and Father... May the God of hope fill you with all joy and peace as you trust in him, so that you may overflow with hope by the power of the Holy Spirit.

Taken from Rom 16:25-27 (TLB)
I commit you to God, who is able to make you strong and steady ....this message is being preached everywhere, so that people ALL around the world will have faith in Christ ... Amen.

~~~~~~~

1 CORINTHIANS is the first of two letters written by Paul to the church at Corinth (a city in Ancient Greece). Approximate date of writing: 53-57 AD

Purpose of writing:
To confront and correct problems that had arisen among the believers in Corinth. Paul corrects wrong thinking, encourages unity but confronts inappropriate behaviour within the church. He reminds his readers of the death and resurrection of Christ, and encourages people to live a life that honours God on our journey through this world.

Overall theme of chapters:

- 1-4 ~ Overcoming conflicts / Learning God's Way
- 5-6 ~ Confronting immorality and disputes in the church
- 7-11 ~ Answering questions raised by the Corinthians
- 11-14 ~ Order in worship / God works by His Spirit / The power of 'God's Kind of Love'
- 15 ~ The Resurrection of Christ / our future resurrection
- 16 ~ Closing words
~~~~~~~

Some key verses

Taken from 1 Cor 1:10, 3:17, 4:20 (The Message)
Learn to be considerate of one another, cultivating a life in common....you are the temple of God, and God himself is present in you...God's Way is not a matter of mere talk; it's an empowered life.

Taken from 1 Cor 6:11-12+19 (GNT)
You have been purified from sin.... you have been put right with God by the Lord Jesus Christ and by the Spirit of our God..... Someone will say, "I am allowed to do anything." Yes; but not everything is good for you.....your body is the temple of the Holy Spirit, who lives in you...

Taken from 1 Cor 11:23-25 (from The Message)
Jesus, on the night of his betrayal, took bread. Having given thanks, he broke it and said, "This is my body, broken for you. Do this to remember me." After supper, he did the same thing with the cup: "This cup is my blood, my new covenant with you. Each time you drink this cup, remember me."

Taken from 1 Cor 12:4-6 (NIV)
There are different kinds of gifts, but the same Spirit distributes them. There are different kinds of service, but the same Lord. There are different kinds of working, but in all of them and in everyone it is the same God at work.

Taken from 1 Cor 13:4-7
Love is patient and kind. Love is not jealous or boastful or proud or rude. It does not demand its own way. It is not irritable, and it keeps no record of being wronged. It does not rejoice about injustice but rejoices whenever the truth wins out. Love never gives up, never loses faith, is always hopeful, and endures through every circumstance.

Taken from 1 Cor 15:3-4+20 (TLB)
Christ died for our sins just as the (Old Testament) *Scriptures said he would...he was buried... three days afterwards he arose from the grave just as the prophets foretold... Christ did actually rise from the dead and has become the first of millions who will come back to life again someday...*

Taken from 1 Cor 15:42-44 (from GNT)
This is how it will be when the dead are raised to life. When the body is buried, it is mortal; when raised, it will be immortal. When buried, it is weak; when raised, it will be strong. When buried, it is a physical body; when raised, it will be a spiritual body.

Taken from 1 Cor 16:13-14 (GNT)
Be alert, stand firm in the faith, be brave, be strong. Do all your work in love.

~~~~~~~

2 CORINTHIANS is the second letter by Paul to the church at Corinth. Approximate date of writing: 55-57AD

Purpose of writing:
Paul continues to confront problems in the church and encourages his readers to remember who they are in Christ. He urges them to persevere despite troubles or persecution.

Overall theme of chapters:
- 1-7 ~ Comfort in God / Sharing Good News
- 8-9 ~ Grace, Generosity and our Position in Christ
- 10-13 ~ Insight into the Apostolic Ministry and Final Greetings
~~~~~~~

Some key verses:

Taken from 2 Cor 1:3-4
God is our merciful Father and the source of all comfort. He comforts us in all our troubles so that we can comfort others. When they are troubled, we will be able to give them the same comfort God has given us.

Taken from 2 Cor 3:1-3 (The Message)
Your lives are a letter that anyone can read by just looking at you. Christ himself wrote it—not with ink, but with God's living Spirit; not chiseled into stone, but carved into human lives

Taken from 2 Cor 4:5-9+16-17 (NCV)
We do not preach about ourselves, but we preach that Jesus Christ is Lord ....God once said, "Let the light shine out of the darkness!" This is the same God who made his light shine in our hearts by letting us know the glory of God that is in the face of Christ.....
We have this treasure from God, but we are like clay jars that hold the treasure. This shows that the great power is from God, not from us. We have troubles....but we are not defeated. We do not know what to do but we do not lose hope..... God does not leave us....so we do not give up
Our physical body is becoming older...but our spirit inside us is made new every day. We have an eternal glory that is much greater than the troubles.

Taken from 2 Cor 5:17-21 (NIV)
If anyone is in Christ, the new creation has come: The old has gone, the new is here! .... God was reconciling the world to himself in Christ, not counting people's sins against them. And he has committed to us the message of reconciliation...God made him who had no sin to be sin for us, so that in him we might become the righteousness of God.

Taken from 2 Cor 13:14 (NIV)
May the grace of the Lord Jesus Christ and the love of God, and the fellowship of the Holy Spirit be with you all.

~~~~~~~

GALATIANS was written by Paul to the church in Galatia (an ancient region in Asia Minor). Approximate date of writing: 53-54 AD.

Purpose of writing:
To address legalistic thinking within the church, where some people thought they had to 'earn' God's acceptance by doing 'good works' rather than by simply receiving His Love and Grace. Paul urges his readers to continue to live in the freedom that Christ has given them, to do good.

Overall theme of chapters:
- 1-2 ~ Paul describes his own time of legalistic thinking before receiving God's Grace (as an example)
- 3-4 ~ We are God's children by faith (united in Christ)
- 5-6 ~ We are free in Christ, not slaves to religious law

Some key verses:

Taken from Gal 2:20-21 (from The Message)
What actually took place is this: I tried keeping rules and working my head off to please God, and it didn't work. So I quit being a "law man" so that I could be God's man...Christ's life showed me how, and enabled me to do it. I identified myself completely with him. Indeed, I have been 'crucified with Christ'. My ego is no longer central....Christ lives in me. The life you see me living is not "mine," but it is lived by faith in the Son of God, who loved me and gave himself for me. I am not going to go back on that.
~~~~~~~

Taken from Gal 3:26-28 (GNT)
It is through faith that all of you are God's children in union with Christ Jesus. You were baptized into union with Christ, and now you are clothed, so to speak, with the life of Christ himself. So there is no difference between Jews and Gentiles, between slaves and free people, between men and women; you are all one in union with Christ Jesus.

Taken from Gal 5:1+6 (NIV) and Gal 5:22-23
It is for freedom that Christ has set us free. Stand firm, then, and do not let yourselves be burdened again by a yoke of slavery. .... The only thing that counts is faith expressing itself through love....The Holy Spirit produces this kind of fruit in our lives: love, joy, peace, patience, kindness, goodness, faithfulness, gentleness, and self-control. There is no law against these things!

~~~~~~~

EPHESIANS was written by Paul to the church in Ephesus (a city in Asia Minor) while he was under house arrest in Rome. Approximate date of writing: 60-62 AD.

Purpose of writing:
To teach more about being 'in Christ'; to help people understand how much God The Father loves them; and encourage them to love one another.

Paul encourages husbands and wives to show love and respect to oneanother. He goes on to explain that marriage lived in this way presents an insight of the relationship between Christ and His Church. For example: In His Love, Christ ('The Bridegroom') laid down everything He had for The Church ('His Bride') ~ and The Church, in her love honours Christ. 'Love and respect' working together.
~~~~~~~

Overall theme of chapters:

- 1-3 ~ What God has done for us
- 4-5 ~ Principles to live by (including in marriage)
- 6 ~ Further advice and the Spiritual Battle

Some key verses:

Taken from Eph 1:4-5 / Eph 3:6
Even before he made the world, God loved us and chose us in Christ to be holy and without fault in his eyes. God decided in advance to adopt us into his own family by bringing us to himself through Jesus Christ. This is what he wanted to do, and it gave him great pleasure....And this is God's plan: Both Gentiles and Jews who believe the Good News share equally in the riches inherited by God's children. Both are part of the same body, and both enjoy the promise of blessings because they belong to Christ Jesus.

Taken from Eph 5:21-28 (NIV/The Message)
Submit to one another out of reverence for Christ....
Wives, understand and support your husbands in ways that show your support for Christ. The husband provides leadership to his wife the way Christ does to his church, not by domineering but by cherishing. So just as the church submits to Christ as he exercises such leadership, wives should likewise submit to their husbands.....
Husbands, go all out in your love for your wives, exactly as Christ did for the church—a love marked by giving, not getting. Christ's love makes the church whole. His words evoke her beauty. Everything he does and says is designed to bring the best out of her, dressing her in dazzling white silk, radiant with holiness. And that is how husbands ought to love their wives. They're really doing themselves a favor—since they're already "one" in marriage....

No one abuses his own body, does he? No, he feeds and pampers it. That's how Christ treats us, the church, since we are part of his body. And this is why a man leaves father and mother and cherishes his wife. No longer two, they become "one flesh." This is a huge mystery, and I don't pretend to understand it all. What is clearest to me is the way Christ treats the church. And this provides a good picture of how each husband is to treat his wife, loving himself in loving her, and how each wife is to honor her husband.

Taken from Eph 6:1-18 (NCV)
Children, honor your father and mother....Fathers, do not make your children angry, but raise them with the training and teaching of the Lord.

....Work as if you were serving the Lord, not as if you were serving only men and women.... be strong in the Lord and in his great power. Put on the full armor of God so that you can fight against the devil's evil tricks. Our fight is not against people on earth but against the rulers and authorities and the powers of this world's darkness, against the spiritual powers of evil in the heavenly world. That is why you need to put on God's full armor. Then on the day of evil you will be able to stand strong. And when you have finished the whole fight, you will still be standing.

...So stand strong, with the belt of truth tied around your waist and the protection of right living on your chest. On your feet wear the Good News of peace to help you stand strong. And also use the shield of faith with which you can stop all the burning arrows of the Evil One. Accept God's salvation as your helmet, and take the sword of the Spirit, which is the word of God. Pray in the Spirit at all times with all kinds of prayers, asking for everything you need. To do this you must always be ready and never give up. Always pray for all God's people.

~~~~~~~

PHILIPPIANS is a letter written by Paul to the church in Philippi (a city in Ancient Macedonia). Approximate date of writing: 60-62 AD.

Purpose of writing:
To say 'Thank-you' to the Philippians for their love, help and support; to encourage them in their spiritual walk and urge his readers to follow Christ's example in their lives.

Overall theme of chapters:

- 1 ~ Paul encourages his readers
- 2 ~ Having the mind of Christ
- 3 ~ Having confidence in Him
- 4 ~ Having peace through Him

Some key verses

Taken from Phil 1:6 / Phil 2:5-7 (NIV)
I am certain that God, who began the good work within you, will continue his work until it is finally finished on the day when Christ Jesus returns...... In your relationships with one another, have the same mindset as Christ Jesus: Who, being in very nature God, did not consider equality with God something to be used to his own advantage; rather, he made himself nothing by taking the very nature of a servant, being made in human likeness.

Taken from Phil 3:14 (NIV) / Phil 4:6-7 (NCV)
I press on toward the goal to win the prize for which God has called me heavenward in Christ Jesus.... So do not worry about anything, but pray and ask God for everything you need, always giving thanks. And God's peace, which is so great we cannot understand it, will keep your hearts and minds in Christ Jesus.
~~~~~~~

~~~~~~~

COLOSSIANS is a letter written by Paul to the church in Colossae (a city near Laodicea, about 100 miles from Ephesus in Asia Minor). Approximate time of writing: 60-62 A.D.

Purpose of writing:
Paul encourages the Colossians to keep their hearts and minds on God, and focus on Christ. Paul tells his readers that Jesus Himself is the completeness of God; he urges people to avoid strife, and to live in peace with one another.

Overall theme of chapters:
- 1-2 ~ The Supremacy of Christ
- 3-4 ~ Living in Him

Some key verses:

Taken from Col 1:15-20 (NCV)
No one can see God, but Jesus Christ is exactly like him. He ranks higher than everything that has been made. Through his power all things were made—things in heaven and on earth, things seen and unseen... All things were made through Christ and for Christ. He was there before anything was made, and all things continue because of him. He is the head of the body, which is the church. Everything comes from him. He is the first one who was raised from the dead. So in all things Jesus has first place. God was pleased for all of himself to live in Christ. And through Christ, God has brought all things back to himself again—things on earth and things in heaven.

Taken from Col 2:9-10 (NLV) / Col 3:13-15 (TLB)
For Christ is God in human flesh....When you have Christ, you are complete....so be gentle and ready to forgive... Remember, the Lord forgave you.... let love guide your life and the peace of heart that comes from Christ...Always be thankful.
~~~~~~~

~~~~~~~

1 THESSALONIANS is the first of two letters written by Paul to the church in Thessalonica (an ancient city in Northern Greece) Approximate time of writing: 51-52 AD.

Purpose of writing:
To strengthen and encourage, focusing on the principles of Faith, Hope and Love. Paul reminds his readers that God is at work in and through them here and now, and that He is with them for all eternity.

Overall theme of chapters:
- 1-3 ~ Paul's personal thanks and reflections
- 4-5 ~ Paul's instructions to the Thessalonians

Some key verses:

Taken from 1 Thess 2:13 (GNT) 1 Thess 3:12-13 (NIV)
We always give thanks to God...who is at work in you... May the Lord make your love increase and overflow for each other and for everyone else...May he strengthen your hearts...

Taken from 1 Thess 5:16-17 (GNT) / 1 Thess 5:23
Be joyful always, pray at all times, be thankful in all circumstances...May the God of peace make you holy in every way, and may your whole spirit and soul and body be kept blameless until our Lord Jesus Christ comes again.

~~~~~~~

2 THESSALONIANS is the second letter written by Paul to the church in Thessalonica. Approximate time of writing: 51-52 AD (believed to be written several months after 1 Thessalonians).

Purpose of writing:
To encourage his readers to persevere and to hold on to what is true; to emphasize the future return of Jesus Christ, as there were some people in Thessalonica who were saying that Jesus had already returned, so this letter was sent to correct misleading information.

Overall theme of chapters:
- 1-2 ~ Paul speaks again about Jesus' return
- 3 ~ Paul encourages and comforts his readers

Some key verses:

Taken from 2 Thess 2:1-2+16-17 / 2 Thess 3:3+5 (NIV)
Now, dear brothers and sisters, let us clarify some things about the coming of our Lord Jesus Christ and how we will be gathered to meet him. Don't be so easily shaken or alarmed by those who say that the day of the Lord has already begun. Now may our Lord Jesus Christ himself and God our Father, who loved us and by his grace gave us eternal comfort and a wonderful hope, comfort you and strengthen you in every good thing you do and say....The Lord is faithful, and he will strengthen you and protect you from the evil one.....May the Lord direct your hearts into God's love and Christ's perseverance.

~~~~~~~

1 TIMOTHY was written as the first of two Pastoral letters from Paul to a man named Timothy. Approximate date of writing: 60-65 AD.

Purpose of writing:
To encourage Timothy who was a young Pastor at the church in Ephesus; to give Timothy instructions and guidelines to follow in his leadership role.
~~~~~~~

Overall theme of chapters:

- 1-2 ~ Instructions to Timothy
- 4-5 ~ Guidelines for good leadership

Some key verses:

Taken from 1 Tim 2:1-5 (GNT)
I urge that petitions, prayers, requests, and thanksgivings be offered to God for all people; for kings and all others who are in authority, that we may live a quiet and peaceful life with all reverence toward God and with proper conduct. This is good and it pleases God our Savior, who wants everyone to be saved and to come to know the truth. For there is one God, and there is one who brings God and human beings together, the man Christ Jesus.

Taken from 1 Tim 5:1-3+21+25
Never speak harshly to an older man, but appeal to him respectfully as you would to your own father. Talk to younger men as you would to your own brothers. Treat older women as you would your mother, and treat younger women with all purity as you would your own sisters. Take care of any widow who has no one else to care for her.
Do not show favouritism to anyone..... the good deeds of some people are obvious.....And the good deeds done in secret will someday come to light.

~~~~~~~

2 TIMOTHY is the second Pastoral letter from Paul to Timothy. Approximate date of writing: 65-66 AD.

After his last missionary journey (believed to be into Spain), Paul was again put into prison during the reign of the Roman Emperor Nero.
~~~~~~~

Paul's second letter to Timothy is believed to have been written during that time and therefore his last letter chronologically.

Purpose of writing:
To give Timothy direction; Paul knew his ministry was nearly complete and he wanted to strengthen Timothy to press on in his own life and ministry.

Overall theme of chapters:
- 1 ~ Confidence in God, despite circumstances
- 2-4 ~ Encouragement and instructions to Timothy

Some key verses:
Taken from 2 Tim 1:7 (NIV) / 2 Tim 2:2 / 2 Tim 4:2 (NCV)
The Spirit God gave us does not make us timid, but gives us power, love and self-discipline....Now teach these truths to other trustworthy people who will be able to pass them on to others. Preach the Good News. Be ready at all times... Encourage them with great patience and careful teaching

~~~~~~~

TITUS is another Pastoral letter from Paul to a church leader. Approximate date of writing: 61-63 AD.

Purpose of writing:
To encourage and guide a church leader named 'Titus' (a Greek believer) in his leadership of the churches in Crete. Paul counsels Titus and gives advice on how to deal with difficult situations, including opposition.

Overall theme of chapters:
- 1 ~ The appointment of Elders and Leaders
- 2-3 ~ The importance of sound doctrine
~~~~~~~

Some key verses:

Taken from Titus 2:11 / Titus 3:4-5 / Titus 3:9 (NIV)
For the grace of God has been revealed, bringing salvation to all people....God our Savior revealed his kindness and love.. not because of the righteous things we had done, but because of his mercy. He washed away our sins, giving us a new birth and new life through the Holy Spirit....avoid controversies, arguments and quarrels because these are unprofitable and useless.

~~~~~~~

PHILEMON is another letter written by Paul while he was in prison, to a man named Philemon. Approximate date of writing : 60-62 AD.

Purpose of writing:
To encourage Philemon to forgive a man named Onesimus (who was a servant of Philemon, and a new believer in Christ). It appears Onesimus had run away from Philemon's service ~ at that time this was a crime for which the servant could have been executed under Roman Law. But Paul asks Philemon to show forgiveness to Onesimus and to welcome him back as a brother in Christ.

Overall theme of chapter:
- 1 ~ Forgiveness

Some key verses:

Taken from Philemon 1:6 / Philemon 1:25 (AMP)
I am praying that you will put into action the generosity that comes from your faith as you understand and experience all the good things we have in Christ....The grace of the Lord Jesus Christ be with your spirit.
~~~~~~~

Section Five

INTRODUCING THE NEW TESTAMENT LETTERS WHICH OFFER INSIGHT FOR ALL GENERATIONS

New Testament Letters (part 2)

INTRODUCING THE NEW TESTAMENT LETTERS (Part 2)

Letters written by James, Peter, John, and Jude

(Includes a brief insight into The Book of Revelation)

The Books are listed below as they appear in The New Testament. For chronological order please see timeline in section six.

HEBREWS was a general letter written primarily to the Hebrew believers of the time. The writer of this letter is unknown, although some Scholars believe the letter could have been written by Paul or Barnabas. It is dated approximately 63-67 AD.

Purpose of writing

To show that Jesus is more than an angel; He is the perfect likeness of God Himself. To show that the New Covenant Christ made (through His Work at The Cross) is greater than the Old Covenant of rituals and religious law-keeping.

The author encouragers his readers to recognise that the Old Testament showed mankind's need for a Saviour, and that 'rituals' and 'religious laws' were given to offer a temporary solution to sin until the time that Jesus came.

The writer shows how the Old Testament gave illustrations ('types' or 'shadows') which pointed to the real thing, Christ Himself (who paid for all sin, for all time).

Overall theme of chapters:

- 1-4 ~ The Supremacy of Jesus
- 5-8 ~ The Priesthood of Christ
- 9-10 ~ His Perfect Sacrifice
- 11-13 ~ Encouragement to look to Him

Some key verses:

Taken from Heb 1:1-2 (NIV)
In the past God spoke to our ancestors through the prophets at many times and in various ways, but in these last days he has spoken to us by his Son, whom he appointed heir of all things, and through whom also he made the universe. The Son is the radiance of God's glory and the exact representation of his being, sustaining all things by his powerful word.

Taken from Heb 7:24-27
....because Jesus lives forever, he has a permanent priesthood. Therefore he is able to save completely those who come to God through him, because he always lives to intercede for them. Such a high priest truly meets our need—one who is holy, blameless....exalted above the heavens. Unlike the other high priests, he does not need to offer sacrifices day after day, first for his own sins, and then for the sins of the people. He sacrificed for their sins once for all when he offered himself.

Taken from Heb 9:11 / Heb 10:12
So Christ has now become the High Priest over all the good things that have come. He has entered that greater, more perfect Tabernacle in heaven, which was not made by human hands and is not part of this created world....... He offered himself to God as a single sacrifice for sins, good for all time. Then he sat down in the place of honor at God's right hand.

Taken from Heb 11:1 / Heb 12:1-2 / Heb 13:8 (NCV)
Faith means being sure of the things we hope for and knowing that something is real even if we do not see it....We are surrounded by a great cloud of people whose lives tell us what faith means. So let us run the race that is before us and never give up.....Let us look to Jesus... He is the same yesterday, today, and forever.

~~~~~~~

JAMES is a letter written by the half-brother of Jesus (named James). It is believed to be the first New Testament letter to be written (chronologically) by an Apostle, and dated approximately 46-50 AD.

Purpose of writing:
It was written primarily to Jewish believers to encourage them to love and persevere while going through persecution. James gives advice on practical Christian living and offers guidance for a life of faith.

Overall theme of chapters:
- 1~ 3 Faith, Wisdom and Love
- 4~ 5 Giving yourself to God

Some key verses:

Taken from James 1:5+17 (NIV) / James 2:23 (NLV)
....If any of you lacks wisdom....ask God, who gives generously to all without finding fault, and it will be given to you... For every good and perfect gift is from above, coming down from the Father of the heavenly lights, who does not change like shifting shadows... Abraham put his trust in God and he became right with God, he was called the friend of God
~~~~~~~

Taken from James 3:17 (GNT)
The wisdom from above is first of all pure. It is also peace loving, gentle at all times, and willing to yield to others. It is full of mercy and the fruit of good deeds. It shows no favoritism and is always sincere.

Taken from James 4:7-8 / James 5:16 (The Message)
So let God work his will in you. Yell a loud no to the Devil and watch him scamper. Say a quiet yes to God and he'll be there in no time....The prayer of a person living right with God is something powerful to be reckoned with.

~~~~~~~

1 PETER is the first of two general letters written by the Apostle Peter. Approximate date of writing: 62-63 AD.

Purpose of writing:
To encourage his readers to live a godly lifestyle, and to endure even during times of suffering and persecution. Peter reminds people that Christ took our sin, encourages his readers to stand firm, and to walk in God's Love.

Overall theme of chapters:
- 1-3 ~ Salvation for all who believe
- 4-5 ~ Continue in His Love

Some key verses:

Taken from 1 Peter 1:3-5 (The Message)
What a God we have!...Because Jesus was raised from the dead, we've been given a brand-new life and have everything to live for, including a future in heaven—and the future starts now! God is keeping careful watch over us and the future. The Day is coming when you'll have it all—life healed and whole...
~~~~~~~

Taken from 1 Peter 2:24 / 1 Peter 3:22 (NCV)
Christ carried our sins in his body on the cross so we would stop living for sin and start living for what is right. And you are healed because of his wounds....Now Jesus has gone into heaven and is at God's right-side ruling over angels, authorities, and powers.

Taken from 1 Peter 4:8 / 1 Peter 5:7
Continue to show deep love for each other, for love covers a multitude of sins....Give all your worries and cares to God, for he cares about you.

~~~~~~~

2 PETER is the second of the two general letters written by the Apostle Peter. Approximate date of writing: 63-65 AD.

Purpose of writing:
To encourage his readers to keep on believing, and keep on trusting Jesus. Peter also warns his readers to be on their guard against teaching that denied the Divinity of Christ, and was disruptive or based on fear rather than the Patience and Grace of God.

Overall theme of chapters:
- 1 ~ The Power of God
- 2 ~ 3 ~ Do not be deceived

Some key verses:

Taken from 2 Peter 1:3-4+16
God has given us everything we need for living a godly life...by knowing him....and he has given us great and precious promises...for we were not making up clever stories when we told you about the powerful coming of our Lord Jesus Christ. We saw his majestic splendor with our own eyes..
~~~~~~~

Taken from 2 Peter 3:17-18 (AMP)
Be on your guard so that you are not carried away by the error of unprincipled men who distort doctrine.... but grow in the grace and knowledge of our Lord and Savior Jesus Christ. To Him be glory, both now and to the day of eternity. Amen.

~~~~~~~

1 JOHN is the first of three general letters written by the Apostle John, to all believers. Approximate date of writing: 80-90 AD.

Purpose of writing:
To assure his readers of The Life and Love of Christ; to encourage them to love oneanother, and to live a lifestyle that was appropriate for people guided by God's Light. John also confronts erroneous teachings (for example, teaching from some sources were denying Jesus had a genuine human body).

Overall theme of chapters:

- 1-2 ~ A reminder of who Jesus is
- 4-5 ~ A call to love oneanother and reassurance

Some key verses:

Taken from 1 John 1:1-3 (NLV) 1 John 4:7, 5:13 (NIV)
Christ is the Word of Life. He was from the beginning. We have heard Him and have seen Him with our own eyes. We have looked at Him and put our hands on Him. Christ, Who is Life, was shown to us. We saw Him. We tell you and preach about the Life that lasts forever. He was with the Father and He has come down to us. Dear friends, let us love one another, for love comes from God. Everyone who loves has been born of God and knows God.... I write these things to you who believe in the name of the Son of God so that you may know that you have eternal life.
~~~~~~~

~~~~~~~

2 JOHN is the second of three general letters by John; it was written to a church which he refers to as 'lady'. John is believed to have been the Elder and wrote this letter while he was in Ephesus. Approximate date of writing: 80-90 AD.

Purpose of writing:
To encourage his readers not to lose their focus on Jesus and to walk in God's Love. John also continues to confront any false notions that deny Jesus had appeared as a man, in a fully human body.

Instead, he encourages his readers to keep their focus on 'The Truth'. As a cross reference: in John's Gospel, he recorded the words of Jesus who said: "I AM The Truth, The Way and The Life" (John 14:6)

Overall theme of chapter:

- Truth and Love

Some key verses:

Taken from 2 John 1:3 (NIV)
Grace, mercy and peace from God the Father and from Jesus Christ, the Father's Son, will be with us in truth and love.

Taken from 2 John 1: 5-6 (NCV)
I ask you that we all love each other. And love means living the way God commanded us to live. As you have heard from the beginning, his command is this: Live a life of love.

~~~~~~~

3 JOHN is the third general letter by John, this time written to a man named Gaius, who lived in Ephesus. Approximate date of writing: 80-90 AD.

Purpose of writing:
To encourage his friend, and encourage others, to keep doing good and reject evil.

Overall theme of chapter:
- Walk in The Truth

Some key verses:

Taken from 3 John 1:4+11 (GNT)
Nothing makes me happier than to hear that my children live in the truth... My dear friend, do not imitate what is bad, but imitate what is good. Whoever does good belongs to God; whoever does what is bad has not seen God.

~~~~~~~

JUDE is a general letter written by Jude, the brother of James (both of these men were half-brothers of Jesus). Approximate date of writing: around 65-80 AD.

Purpose of writing:
To give an illustration of good teaching, compared to some of the erroneous ideas that were circulating at the time.

Overall theme of chapter:
- Stay in Faith / Keep Trusting Jesus

Some key verses:

Taken from Jude 1:1b-2 (NCV)
God the Father loves you, and you are kept safe in Jesus Christ: Mercy, peace, and love be yours richly.
~~~~~~~

Taken from Jude 1:24-25 (NIV)
To him who is able to keep you from stumbling and to present you before his glorious presence without fault and with great joy— to the only God our Savior be glory, majesty, power and authority, through Jesus Christ our Lord, before all ages, now and forevermore! Amen.

~~~~~~~

REVELATION is a prophetic letter written by the Apostle John, in his elderly years, while he was a prisoner on the Island of Patmos. Approximate date of writing: 85-90 A.D.

Purpose of writing:
To share with his readers a Revelation of The Risen Christ; to give encouragement and hope that Jesus will return to earth one day and that 'every eye will see Him'.

John warns of incredible circumstances that the earth will experience before He comes back. The visionary nature of the writing means it is shrouded in symbolism (often looking from Heaven's perspective) which is meant to inspire not to cause fear and dread.

The visions John records for us show that Heavenly battles are often taking place, which can relate to events on the earth. However, no one can know the exact meaning of it all. That is why it is important not try and interpret the Scriptures through our own natural thinking or ideas.

The intention of Revelation has always been to bring hope, by reminding us that despite difficult times God is at work (often unseen by us), and that He is making 'all things new' in both heaven and on earth.
~~~~~~~

A Simple Overview of The Book of Revelation:

In Chapter 1, John describes a remarkable vision of The Risen Christ. Jesus speaks with John during the vision, and instructs him to write a letter to seven churches from The Lord Himself.

Chapters 2 to 3 tell us the message of the letters to the churches, from which there is much we can learn today. Through Chapter 4 to Chapter 20, John tells his readers what he sees in his continued vision (which is taking place from the ***perspective of the spiritual realm***).

John describes Jesus as 'The Lamb of God who was slain' (referring to The Cross), and 'The Lamb who is Worthy'. John writes about a vision of a Scroll with 'Seven Seals' and says that only Jesus is worthy to open it and reveal its contents.

John goes on to see visions of 'Seven Angels' (holding 'Seven Trumpets') and a great spiritual battle taking place, which continues with another 'Seven Angels' carrying 'Seven Bowls'.

The text can be difficult to understand but we need to remember that it is visionary and written in a ***language of imagery*** ~ *Section 7 offers a simple insight into some of The Bible's symbolism that can be used in visions and prophetic scripture.*

This incredible book was written at the time to people who would have understood the imagery. They would have been able to relate to similarities in the Old Testament, and seen the deeper meaning.

Today, in our modern and western world, much of the images used can sound perplexing. However, the writing as a whole has eternal insight from which we can all be encouraged.

It is generally believed that some the events that Revelation refers to have taken place, and some have not. The book was written to point us to Christ, rather to cause people to try to figure out dates and times of events.

There are many things we are not told, so as to avoid such complications. The main focus is the overcoming power of Jesus in all things, both in Heaven and on earth. We are simply meant to observe the times and seasons, and know that Jesus will return as he has promised.

We also need to remember that the spiritual battles are waged against God's enemies. We need to keep in or minds and hearts that Jesus came to earth to redeem mankind, so that all people who put faith in Him become ***'Friends of God'*** (John 15:15).

The writing shows that ***in Christ we overcome the battles we face by leaning on Him***, and that one day He will return. This is meant to inspire us ~ God is always working on our behalf in the background, often unseen by us. This is especially good to know when we are facing difficult times.

God is faithful, and He is working something out that we do not always understand, but He can be trusted in all things. We need The Holy Spirit to speak to our hearts in His Love and Care. God is for us not against us; He wants us to put our hope in Christ, who loves us (Rom 8:31-38).

John's imagery refers to Jesus through terms such as 'The Lamb' *(sacrifice)*; 'The Lion of Judah' *(deliverer)*; 'The Rider on The White Horse' *(rescuer)* and 'The Bridegroom' *(Husband of The Church, showing the personal relationship He desires with each of us).*

John's imagery also reveals an eternal 'hell' which was made for God's enemies (in other words: Satan ~ who is referred to in picture language as things like the 'Dragon' / 'Beast').

The Church (which is made up of all believers everywhere, across all time) is referred to as a 'woman' and 'The Bride of The Lamb'. It is also the 'Golden Lampstand' which Jesus holds in His Hands, as described in Chapter 1.

The writing is meant to point people to the truth that God welcomes all who trust in Jesus to enter The Courts of Heaven (His Eternal Presence). Evil and suffering cannot gain entrance in Heaven's eternity, where God promises to ***'wipe away every tear from our eyes'*** (Rev 21:4).

John describes different periods of time within his writing, which are subject to the 'picture language' nature of the Book of Revelation. Therefore, it is probable that many of the numbers he uses also have a deeper meaning. We must be wary of taking the 'picture' or 'number' language too literally in visions or prophetic writings.

John goes on to tell us that a time will come where Jesus 'Reigns upon the earth', and the evil one is cast into a 'Lake of Fire'. In Chapters 21 to 22, John describes the ***New Heaven and New Earth*** where there is ***no more death, no more sickness, no pain, no mourning or crying***.

The writing is telling us that the present order of things (along with the troubles that we experience today) will one day pass away. John completes his writing by telling us that ***'God is making all things new'***.

So, let's keep in mind that Revelation is meant to inspire and encourage us, not to frighten or bemuse. It is to give us hope, and to know that God is with us throughout all things, both now and forever (Matt 1:23 / Matt 28:18-20).

Main focus of each chapter:

- 1 ~ Revelation of The Person of Jesus
- 2 ~ Letters to The Churches in Ephesus, Smyrna, Pergamum, and Thyatira
- 3 ~ Letters to The Churches in Sardis, Philadelphia and Laodicea
- 4 ~ Vision of The Heavenly Throne
- 5 ~ Vision of 'The Scroll with Seven Seals' and 'The Lamb who is Worthy'
- 6 ~ Vision of the opening of the first six seals
- 7 ~ Vision of The Great Crowd before God
- 8 ~ Vision of the opening of the seventh seal
- 9 ~ Vision of troubles and distress
- 10 ~ Vision of an Angel with a Small Scroll
- 11 ~ Vision of Two Witnesses and The Temple
- 12 ~ Vision of The Woman and her offspring. The Dragon (Satan) is thrown down from Heaven, and the Woman is persecuted *(the woman here is likely to be referring to God's People under persecution)*
- 13 ~ Vision of a Beast from the Sea and Land
- 14 ~ Vision of The Lamb on Mount Zion
- 15-16 ~ Vision of The Seven Angels
- 17-18 ~ Visions of Evil being Judged

- 19 ~ Visions of Rejoicing in Heaven, The Warrior on The White Horse, Wedding Celebration of The Lamb
- 20 ~ Visions of Satan bound for a time, released, defeated and judged at The Great White Throne
- 21-22 ~ Visions of a New Heaven, New Earth and a New Jerusalem / Paradise will be restored.
- 22 ~ Concludes with a reminder that Jesus is coming back to restore all things, as revealed in this book through imagery and illustration.

Some verses to consider from Revelation:

Taken from Rev 1:4-5+8+10-15+17-18 (TLB)
May you have grace and peace from God who is, and was, and is to come; and from the sevenfold Spirit before his throne; and from Jesus Christ who faithfully reveals all truth to us. He was the first to rise from death, to die no more. He is far greater than any king in all the earth... It was the Lord's Day and I was worshiping, when suddenly I heard a loud voice behind me, a voice that sounded like a trumpet blast, saying, "I am the A and the Z, (the Alpha and The Omega), the Beginning and the Ending of all things!"....

....When I turned to see who was speaking, there behind me were seven candlesticks of gold. And standing among them was one who looked like Jesus, who called himself the Son of Man, wearing a long robe circled with a golden band across his chest. His hair was white as wool or snow, and his eyes penetrated like flames of fire. His feet gleamed like burnished bronze, and his voice thundered like the waves against the shore.... When I saw him, I fell at his feet....but he laid his right hand on me and said, "Don't be afraid! ... I am the First and Last, the Living One who died, who is now alive forevermore.

Taken from Rev 5:13
And then I heard every creature in heaven and on earth and under the earth and in the sea. They sang: "Blessing and honor and glory and power belong to the one sitting on the throne and to the Lamb forever and ever."

Taken from Rev 12:11 (paraphrased by the author)
People overcame troubles and tribulations (for example from the evil one) through faith in Jesus, and by speaking truth and life into their situation...for all eternity is theirs in Christ (even death itself cannot stop our relationship with God).

Taken from Rev 21:1-7+22:17
Then I saw a new heaven and a new earth, for the old heaven and the old earth had disappeared. And the sea was also gone. And I saw the holy city, the new Jerusalem, coming down from God out of heaven like a bride beautifully dressed for her husband. I heard a loud shout from the throne, saying, "Look, God's home is now among his people! He will live with them, and they will be his people. God himself will be with them. He will wipe every tear from their eyes, and there will be no more death or sorrow or crying or pain. All these things are gone forever"....

....And the one sitting on the throne said, "Look, I am making everything new!" And then he said to me, "Write this down, for what I tell you is trustworthy and true." And he also said, "It is finished! I am the Alpha and the Omega—the Beginning and the End. To all who are thirsty I will give freely from the springs of the water of life. All who are victorious will inherit all these blessings, and I will be their God, and they will be my children....The Spirit and the bride say, "Come." Let anyone who hears this say, "Come." Let anyone who is thirsty come. Let anyone who desires drink freely from the water of life.

~~~~~~~
~~~~~~~

Personal Notes

Personal Notes

Section Six

Includes TIMELINE, Acts basic Outline, and notes about Emblems, Fruit and Gifts of the Holy Spirit

REFERENCE NOTES

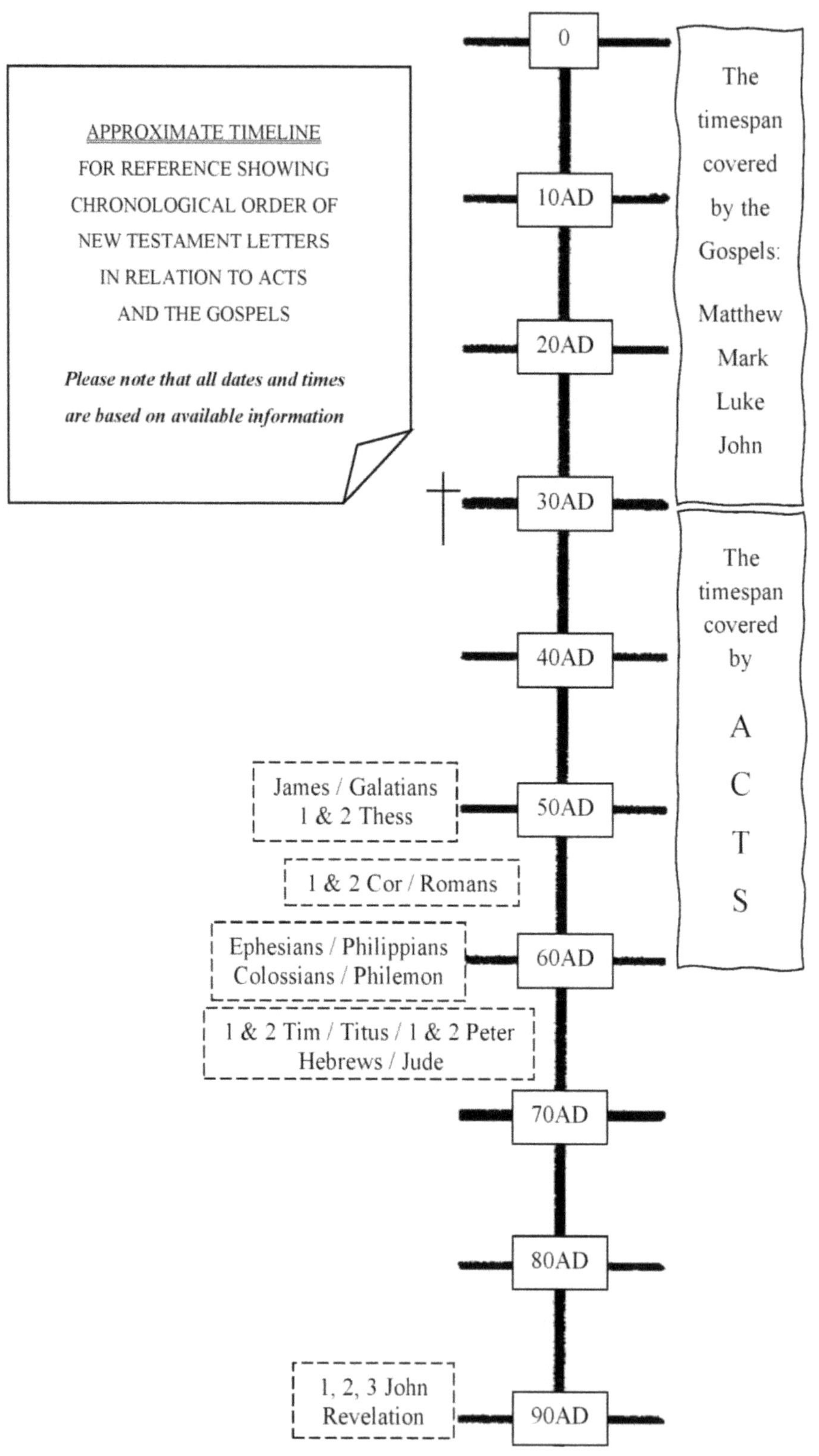
APPROXIMATE TIMELINE
FOR REFERENCE SHOWING
CHRONOLOGICAL ORDER OF
NEW TESTAMENT LETTERS
IN RELATION TO ACTS
AND THE GOSPELS
Please note that all dates and times are based on available information
0
10AD
20AD
30AD
40AD
50AD
60AD
70AD
80AD
90AD
The timespan covered by the Gospels:
Matthew
Mark
Luke
John
The timespan covered by
A
C
T
S
James / Galatians
1 & 2 Thess
1 & 2 Cor / Romans
Ephesians / Philippians
Colossians / Philemon
1 & 2 Tim / Titus / 1 & 2 Peter
Hebrews / Jude
1, 2, 3 John
Revelation

ACTS BASIC OUTLINE

Acts chapters 1 – 4	The Spirit and Birth of The Church
Acts chapters 5 – 7	The Growth of The Church
Acts chapters 8 – 9	Persecution of The Church
Acts chapters 10 – 12	Expansion of The Church
Acts chapters 13 –15	Paul's 1st Missionary Journey
Acts chapters 16 – 18	Paul's 2nd Missionary Journey
Acts chapters 19 – 20	Paul's 3rd Missionary Journey
Acts chapters 21 – 23	Paul's Arrest
Acts chapters 24 – 26	Paul's Trials
Acts chapters 27 – 28	Paul's Imprisonment

Notes about The Jerusalem Council

The **Council of Jerusalem** (also known as the **Meeting at Jerusalem,** the **Apostolic Council** or **Apostolic Decree)** was a meeting of The Apostles and the early church leaders in approximately 50AD.

After prayer, discussion and study, The Meeting decided that non-Jewish believers (Gentile believers) were not obliged to keep The Law of Moses (which was a set of religious instructions given to the Jewish people in The Old Testament).

The Meeting concluded that it is by GOD'S GRACE that people are saved, through FAITH IN JESUS, not by observing religious rituals and practises. (Some people follow them as an expression of their love for God).

The Meeting did give advice to believers for their welfare: to avoid eating meat with blood in it; avoid promiscuity; avoid idolatry; but respect marriage.

Accounts of the Meeting at Jerusalem can be found in Acts chapter 15 and in Paul's Letter to The Galatians (where chapter 2 is believed to be referring to this meeting).

Emblems of the Holy Spirit

- DOVE
  Gentle (Matt 3:16+10:16 / Gal 5:22)
  Guiding (Is 30:21 / John 16:13 / Heb 3:7-11)

- WATER
  To cleanse (Ez 16:9,36:25 / Eph 5:26 / Heb 10:22)
  To grow, nourish (Ps 1:3 / Is 27:3,6+44:3-4)
  To refresh (Ps 46:4 / Is 41:17-18+58:11)
  Given freely (John 3:5, 4:14, 7:37-39 / Rev 22:17)

- RAIN
  Blessing (Ps 133:3+72:6)
  Refreshing (Ps 68:9 / Is 18:5)
  Nourishing (Ez 34:26-27 / Hos 6:3+10:12+14:5)

- WIND
  Unseen but effects are seen (John 3:8)
  Powerful (1 Kings 19:11 / Acts 2:2)
  Renewing (Ez 37:9-10,14)

- FIRE
  To purify (Is 4:4 / Mal 3:2-3)
  To shine light upon (Ex 13:21 / Ps 78:14)
  To examine (Zeph 1:12 / 1 Cor 2:10)
  To empower / give boldness (Acts 2:3,6-11)

- OIL
  Healing (Luke 10:34 / Rev 3:18)
  Comforting (Is 61:3 / Heb 1:9)
  Gives light (Matt 25:3-4 / 1 John 2:20,27)
  Anointing (Ex 29:7, 30:30 / Is 61:1)
  To seal / secure (John 6:27 / 2 Cor 1:22 / Eph 1:13-14+4:30 / Rev 7:2)

- NEW WINE
  New Covenant (Matt 9:16-17 / Rom 11:27 / 1 Cor 11:25)
  Spiritual joy (Neh 8:10b / Eph 5:18 / Rom 15:13)

Fruit of the Holy Spirit

Taken from Gal 5:22-23 (NCV)
The Spirit produces the fruit of ***love, joy, peace, patience, kindness, goodness, faithfulness, gentleness, self-control.*** *There is no law that says these things are wrong.*

1) LOVE is a choice / an act of the will to do good to another (1 Cor 13:1-8)

2) JOY is an inner contentment not dependent on circumstances, whether good or bad (Neh 8:10) / based on God's love and care for the individual

3) PEACE is an inner calmness, passing all understanding (Phil 4:6-7). A quietness of spirit based on The One who is above all the circumstances of life

4) PATIENCE is the capacity to wait / to be able to persevere and continue doing something despite difficulties (James 5:7-11)

5) KINDNESS is being generous and considerate about other people's feelings, over and above your own (Titus 3:4-5)

6) GOODNESS is to have moral conduct that's beneficial to others (Exodus 18:9)

7) FAITHFULNESS is being of trustworthy character / reliable / remaining faithful to someone or something (1 Cor 10:13)

8) GENTLENESS is true strength and power under control / caring but with inner strength and authority (1 Thess 2:7)

9) SELF-CONTROL is limiting and controlling your own feelings and actions in order to display the character of God for His glory (Proverbs 25:28)

Gifts of the Holy Spirit

Taken from 1 Cor 12:4-10
There are different kinds of spiritual gifts, but the same Spirit is the source of them all. There are different kinds of service, but we serve the same Lord. God works in different ways, but it is the same God who does the work in all of us. ***Spiritual gifts*** *are given to each of us so we can help each other.*

To one person the Spirit gives the ability to give ***wise advice****; to another the same Spirit gives a message of* ***special knowledge****. The same Spirit gives* ***great faith*** *to another, and to someone else the one Spirit gives the gift of* ***healing****. He gives one person the power to perform* ***miracles****, and another the ability to* ***prophesy****.*

He gives someone else the ability to ***discern*** *whether a message is from the Spirit of God or from another spirit. Still another person is given the ability to speak in* ***unknown languages****, while another is given the ability to* ***interpret*** *what is being said.*

1) WISDOM ~ beyond our natural understanding
2) KNOWLEDGE ~ beyond our natural knowledge of things
3) FAITH ~ that expects to see healings and miracles
4) HEALING ~ can be an ongoing process (ultimate healing is in eternity)
5) MIRACLES ~ something out of the natural order of things
6) PROPHESY ~ being able to know and share God's heart in a situation
7) DISCERNEMNT ~ ability to distinguish between good and evil spirits
8) TONGUES ~ to speak in an unknown language, never been taught
9) INTERPRETATION ~ to be able to interpret a supernatural tongue

Section Seven

SOME SYMBOLISM USED IN BIBLE VISIONS AND IMAGERY

Bible Symbolism

Some of the Symbolism used in The Bible
with a simplified meaning and some references to consider
(please always think about context of vision / writing)

Ark of the Covenant
The Presence of God
2 Chron 7:1-3

Armour
Spiritual Protection
Rom 13:12 / Eph 6:10-20

Babylon / Beasts
Man-made system of malevolent rule / ungodly people
Dan 7:17 / Revelation 14:8 / 1 Cor 15:32

Banner
Rallying point / A call to come to Jesus (The Root of Jesse)
Is 5:26 / Is 11:10 / Rom 15:12

Brass
Firm / Strong / can symbolise stubbornness
Ps 107:16 / Is 48:4

Candles or Candlesticks (Lampstands)
Symbolic of Churches
Rev 1:20 / Rev 2:1

Chariots
Symbolic of Angelic Hosts
Zech 6:1 / Ps 68:17

Cornerstone
Messiah / Saviour / Christ
Ps 118:22 / Matt 21:42 / Mark 12:10 / Luke 20:17 / Acts 4:11 / 1 Peter 2:7

Crown
Victory over something / a reward
James 1:12 / Rev 2:10

Day
A time period (can be a set time, a past time, or a future time)
Gen 1:5 / Ps 18:18 / 2 Peter 3:8

Door
Opportunity / Freedom
Acts 14:27 / 1 Cor 16:9 / Col 4:3

Dragon
Satan (the devil, the evil one)
Rev 12:3, 9

Eagle
Carried (by God) / Renewed / Strengthened (by trusting God)
Ex 19:4 / Deut. 32:10-11 / Is 40:31 / Ps 103:1-5

Earthquake
Calamity / Chaos
Matt 24:7 / Rev 6:12

Eyes
The heart and mind (how the 'inner person' views things)
Ps 119:18 / Eph 1:18

Forehead
Beliefs / Choices / Mindset
Deut 6:8 / Rev 7:3 / Rev 15:12 / Rev 19:20

Garden
A place of Shelter and Refreshment / God's People / The Church
SOS 4:12 / Is 58:11 / Is 61:11 / Luke 13:19 / John 15:1-8

Gold
Purity / Something of Great Value (can relate to Faith)
1 Peter 1:7 / Rev 3:18

Head
Ruler / Leader
Eph 1:22

Hedge
God's Protection
Job 1:10 / Ez 13:5

Honey
Abundance / Something sought after
Ex 3:8+17 / Lev 20:24 / Rev 10:9-10

Horn
King (or Ruler)
Dan 7:24 / Rev 17:12

Horse
Strength / Power
Ps 147:10-11 / Prov 21:31

Hunger and Thirst
A great desire for something
Matt 5:6 / Luke 1:53

Husband
Jesus (our Spiritual Husband)
Is 54:5 / Is 62:3-5 / Rev 19:7-9

Husbandmen
Leaders / Teachers
Jer31:24 / Matt 21:33

Hyssop
Cleansing
Ps 51:7

Incense
Prayer
Mal 1:11 / Rev 5:8

Keys
Power / Authority / Ability to lock or unlock something
Is 22:22 / Luke 9:1 / Rev 1:18 / Rev 20:1

Lamb of God
Jesus (known as 'The Lamb' referring to His Sacrifice to pay for all sin)
Gen 22:7-8 / John 1:29 / 1 Cor 5:7 / 1 Peter 1:19

Lion of Judah
Jesus (refers to His position as Messiah prophesied by the prophets of Israel, and relates to His Victory over sin and eternal death)
Gen 49:9-10 / John 5:22 / Rev 5:5-10 / Rev 19:11-16

Leaven
Erroneous teaching
Matt 16:12 / 1 Cor 5:6-8

Light
Instruction (guidance) from God and His Word
Ps 27:1 / Ps 119:30 / Prov 6:23 / Matt 5:14

Milk
Abundance / Prosperity
Ez 25:4 / Joel 3:18

Moon
The Church (as the moon reflects the light of the sun, so The Church reflects The Light of Christ)
SOS 6:10 / Ps 89:35-37 / Mal 4:2 / Rev 12:1

Mountains
A kingdom, authority, or rule
Ps 30:7 / Is 2:2 / Dan 2:44-45 / Rev 17:9-11

New Jerusalem
Heavenly City / City of God / Bride of Christ (God's People)
Is 40:9 / Rev 3:12 / Rev 19:7-9 / Rev 21:2+9-10

Night
A time of adversity
Is 21:12 / John 9:4 / Rev 21:25

Oil
Healing / The Holy Spirit / Joy
Gen 37:25 / Matt 25:1-13 / Heb 1:9

Pillar
Upright people / something foundational
Gal 2:9 / 1 Tim 3:15

Rain
Refreshment / Blessing / Holy Spirit
Is 58:11 / Ps 68:9 / Joel 2:23 / Acts 3:20

Rock
God as our refuge and salvation
Ps 18:2 / Ps 94:22 / Ps 95:1

Rod (also measuring rod)
Comfort / Guidance / God's Word
Ps 23:4 / Ecc 12:13 / James 2:10-12

Salt
Purifying / Covenant of friendship / Gracious speech
2 Kings 2:19-22 / Num 18:19 / 2 Chron 13:5 / Matt 5:13

Scroll
A written word (could be God's or man's)
Ezra 6:2 / Jer 36:2 / Ez 3:1-3

Sea
A large number of people
Jer 51:42 / Ez 26:3 / Matt 13:47 / Rev 13:1

Seal / Sealed
Ownership / Security / Protection
Jer 32:11 / Eph 1:13-14 / Eph 4:30

Serpent
Symbolic of something malevolent
Gen 3:1 / Ps 58:4 / 2 Cor 11:3 / Rev 12:9 / Rev 20:2

Sheep
People who follow Jesus (Jesus is 'The Good Shepherd')
Is 40:11 / Luke 15:4 / John 10:11+27

Shepherds
Leaders to guide
Nah 3:18 / Ez 34:2

Shield
Defence / Protection
Ps 84:11 / Eph 6:16

Silver
Redemption / Words of God's truth
Num 18:16 / Ps 12:6

Sleep
In Scripture, can be symbolic of passing on from this world
Dan 12:2, John 11:11, 1 Thess 4:14

Star
Messenger / Angel
Rev 1:16+20

Stars of Heaven
Symbolic of Angelic Beings
Job 38:7

Sword of The Spirit
God's Word
Eph 6:17 / 2 Tim 3:16-18 / 2 Cor 10:4-5 / Heb 4:12

Teeth
Speech ~ *Gal 5:15 / Matt 12:36*
>Gnashing of teeth can represent anger ~ Acts 7:54
>Sometimes can symbolise an attack ~ Job 29:17

Thorns
Troubles / Cares of this world / Sorrow
Prov 24:31 / Matt 13:22 / Mark 15:17

Throne
Seat of government
Ps 122:5 / Dan 7:9

The Tree of Life / The True Vine
A reference to Jesus ('branches' refer to His followers)
John 15:1-8 / Rev 22:1-2 ~ a reference to Eden restored

Trees / Vineyard
Leaders / God's People
Ps 1:3 / Is 55:12 / Is 5:1

Veil
A separation between people and God
Matt 27:51 / Heb 9:3 / Heb 10:20*
***the curtain in The Temple tore from Heaven to earth, when Jesus died on The Cross, signifying The Way to God is now open** (John 14:6)*

Watchman
Prophet
Ez 3:17 / Is 62:6

Water
Symbolic of the Holy Spirit (The Water of Life)
Is 55:1 / John 4:10 / Rev 21:6 / Rev 22:1-2

Waters
In Scripture, when 'waters' is used, it can symbolise afflictions
Ps 69:1 / Is 43:2 {consider context of writing}

Wilderness
A lonely, difficult, or testing time
John 1:23 / Rev 12:6

Wine
Spiritual blessings / Divine Grace / New Covenant
Is 25:6 / Is 65:8-9 / Matt 9:17 / Matt 26:27-28

Wings
Protection / Comfort / Reassurance
Ex 19:4 / Ps 17:8 / Ps 91:4

Woman (women)
In prophesy, a woman can represent a Nation or The Church
(for example: Israel in Rev 12:1 and The Church in Rev 12:17)

Paul spoke symbolically of two 'women' in his letter to the Galatians to represent two types of covenants (Gal 4:21-31)

However, the symbolism of a 'woman' is also used in a negative sense to represent Babylon in Rev 17:5

Therefore, as always, please consider context of writing

Yoke (yoked)
Servanthood / Linked
Jer 5:5 / Matt 11:29–30

Some numbers used in Bible Symbolism
with basic meanings and some references to consider
(please always think about context of vision / writing)

ONE (first) ~ God / Creator / Light / Unity
Gen 1:1+3-5 / Deut 6:4 / John 10:30 /
1 Cor 8:4 / Gal 3:20 / Eph:4-6

TWO (second) ~ Separate / Multiply / Testimony / Witness
Gen 1:6-8+16-17 / Luke 10:1 / John 8:17-18 /
Heb 4:12 / Rev 1:2+Rev 11:3-4

THREE (third) ~ Resurrection / Restoration / Trinity
Hos 6:2 / John 11:25-26 / 1 John 5:7

FOUR (forth, forty) ~ Worldwide
(North, South, East, West) / Authority
Is 11:12 / Ez 37:9 / Rev 4:8 / Rev 7:1

FIVE (fifth) ~ Anoint / Equip / Empower (by God's Grace)
Ex. 30:23-25 / Is 11:2 / Mt. 14:16-21 / Eph 4:11-13

SIX (sixth, 666) ~ The Number of Man
Gen 1:27 / Rev 13:18

SEVEN (seventh) ~ The Number of God /
Perfection / Whole / Complete
Gen 2:3 / Ex 20:11 / Matt 18:21-22 / Heb 4:4

EIGHT (eighth) ~ Reappearance / Return
Rev 17:8,11

NINE (ninth) ~ Fruitfulness / Harvest / Prayer
*Gal. 5:22-23 / 1 Cor. 12:8-10 / Acts 3:1**
(Note: three in the afternoon was known as the ninth hour and a time of prayer)*

TEN (tenth, and multiples of 10) ~
Completeness / Law / Restoration
Deut 4:12-13 / Ex 20:1-17 / Rev 7:4

TWELVE (twelfth, and multiples of 12) ~
Tribes of Israel / God's Rule
Gen 49:28 / Ps 104:19 / Matt 19:28 / Rev 21:12-20

TWENTY-FOUR ~ Perfect Government
Josh 4:2-9 / 1 Kings 19:19 / Rev 4:4-10

SEVENTY ~ Entire / The Whole World
Gen 10

About The Author
And Gardenland Ministries

With Encouragements and Prayer

ABOUT THE AUTHOR AND 'GARDENLAND'

John and Carmel Carberry lead Gardenland Ministries (GLM) inspired by Isaiah 58:11. They were married in 1983 (after becoming Christians in 1982), and have served in church and community life across the years.

While leading a home fellowship in Bedford UK, Carmel began to write easy-to-read books to share with others, initially sharing testimony of dealing with depression and long term illness, and finding steps of healing through faith in Christ. All of her books focus on the Love and Grace of God, and are full of hope and encouragement (which is the heart of GLM).

After John's retirement, they moved to North Derbyshire in 2018. They continue to share articles of faith on their websites and social media, and Carmel's many books can be found at online bookstores, including Amazon, across the world.

GLM's foundational Scriptures: Isaiah 58:11 & Psalm 96:3 say:
"The LORD will guide you always; He will give you water when you are dry and restore your strength. You will be like a well-watered garden, like an ever-flowing spring... Publish His glorious deeds among the nations. Tell everyone about the amazing things God does!"

Please see websites and social media links:

www.gardenlandministries.uk

www.carmelcarberry.com

https://www.facebook.com/CarmelCarberry - Author

https://www.instagram.com/carmelcarberry/

Books by the author (find at Amazon)

THE HIS STORY SERIES

His Story Volume 1 ~ looking at GENESIS

His Story Volume 2 ~ looking at THE GOSPELS

His Story Volume 3 ~ looking at ACTS and the New Testament Letters

His Story Volume 4 ~ seeing CHRIST IN THE OLD TESTAMENT

GARDENLAND BOOKS

God's Fruitful Garden (a book of hope and encouragement)

Communion With God (Soaring on Eagles Wings)

SonRise (Heaven Scent)

SonSet (On The Throne)

SonDown (a taste of Heaven on Earth) ~ includes Bible Studies

Promises (Messages from God's Heart to yours)

Prayers and Blessings (Help in times of need)

Contrast (looks at Bible Covenants and the 'NEW YOU' in Christ)

Our Identity In Christ (a fresh look at our identity in Him)

Any Year Diary *and* Encouragement Notebook (with messages of hope)

LIFE IN THE SPIRIT

Grace Upon Grace
(Prophetic words and visions to encourage and bless in the Grace of God)

Healing Words
(Words to encourage in times of illness)

The Holy Spirit ~ Our Helper and Friend
(Looking at God's Spirit: a simple overview of who He is, what He does, and how He helps us in our lives. includes looking at 'Spiritual Gifts')

Our Beliefs at Gardenland Ministries 

We believe in the authority of Scripture and that Jesus is The Living Word of God (2 Tim 3:16-17 / John 1:1+18 / Heb 1:3)

We believe in Father, Son, and Holy Spirit ~ One God manifest in three persons (Matt 28:18-19 / 2 Cor 13:14)

We believe in the death, burial, and resurrection of Christ, who is now seated in Heaven at the right hand of God (1 Cor 15:3-8 / Mark 16:19-20)

We believe that anyone who puts his/her trust in Jesus is born again and becomes a new creation (Rom 10:9-13 / Rom 3:22 / 2 Cor 5:17)

We believe in the Love and Grace of God, who is full of mercy and compassion to all who come to Him (Psalm 145:8 / Eph 2:4 / Rom 8:1)

We believe in the finished work of Jesus at The Cross and that He paid for all sin for all time (Heb 7:24-25 / Rom 8:34 / Heb 4:16)

We believe that salvation includes healing (Is 53:4-5 / Luke 4:18-19 / 1 Peter 2:24)

We believe that The Holy Spirit fills and empowers believers with supernatural gifts and abilities to do good (Acts 1:8+2:4 / 1 Cor 12:7)

We believe that The Body of Christ spans across all nations and all time, united by God's eternal love (Eph 1:22-23 / Rom 12:5 / 1 Cor 12:27 / John 13:35)

YOU MATTER TO GOD

A Message from God's Heart

I love you so much that I sent My one and only Son, so that through faith in Him you can receive eternal life. I did not send Him to condemn or punish you, I sent Him to rescue you.

All people everywhere have sinned, but I have demonstrated My Love for all people by sending Jesus to die on The Cross to pay for sin forever.

By faith, you can receive My free gift of salvation, for I have already provided it for you, freely by My Grace, and now you simply receive it by putting your trust in Jesus.

When you receive My Son into your heart, a spiritual new birth happens within you ~ you become My Dearly Beloved Child forever, and you become a New Creation!

As you continue to look to My Son day by day, My Holy Spirit will teach and guide you, and I will rejoice over you with singing!

With Eternal Love & Blessing
From your Heavenly Father

Related Bible verses: John 3:16-17 / Rom 3:22-24+5:8 / Eph 2:8 / John 1:12 / 2 Cor 5:17 / John 16:13 / Zeph 3:17

Please say this prayer from your heart if you would like to make Jesus Lord and Saviour of your life.....

PRAYER

Dear Lord Jesus,

Thank You that You have always loved me.

I admit that I have lived my life for myself. I am sorry and repent of my sin.

Thank You that You died on The Cross to save me. I receive the forgiveness that You earned for me.

I believe that You rose from the dead and are now seated at the right hand of The Father.

Please come into my heart to be my Lord and Saviour. Thank You that the moment I asked, You came in, to be with me forever!

Please fill me with Your Holy Spirit and empower me with good gifts to help others. To the honour of Your Name.

Amen

Welcome to the family of God!

John 1:12 (Taken from the Amplified Bible)
All who receive and welcome Him, He gives the right
[the authority, the privilege] to become children of God,
that is, to those who believe in (adhere to, trust in,
and rely on) His name

When you trust in Jesus, The Bible says these things about you....

...you are a new creation (2 Cor 5:17) you are blessed (Eph 1:3) you are God's child (John 1:12) you are redeemed (Eph 1:7-8) you are included in God's eternal plan (Eph 1:13) you have His strength and power living within you (Eph 1:19-21) you are alive in Christ and filled with God's love (Eph 2:4-6) you are seated in Heavenly places with Jesus, spiritually (Eph 2:6) you are 'hand-made' by God, His work of art (Eph 2:10) you have eternal access to God, without fear or shame (Eph 2:17-18) you are part of God's living temple, where He delights to live (Eph 2:21-22) you share in the promises of Christ as one of His heirs (Eph 3:6) you can approach God with freedom and confidence (Eph 3:12) you are being strengthened by Him in your inner being (Eph 3:16) you are loved much more than you can mentally comprehend (Eph 3:18-19) you have His power at work in you to do more than you can imagine (Eph 3:20) you are being built up and equipped for service (Eph 4:11-13) you have favour with God but He has no favourites, all are loved equally (Eph 6:9) you are strong in The Lord and His mighty power (Eph 6:10) you overcome spiritual darkness though His Light and His Word (Eph 6:12-13) you have His truth, righteousness, peace, faith, salvation, Spirit and Word to enable you (Eph 6:14-17) you have the love and peace of Christ within you, forever and for all time (Eph 6:23).

Enjoy these truths and enjoy your new relationship with God!

Personal Notes

Personal Notes

Personal Notes

Personal Notes

Personal Notes

www.ingramcontent.com/pod-product-compliance
Ingram Content Group UK Ltd.
Pitfield, Milton Keynes, MK11 3LW, UK
UKHW051129260726
13967UKWH00010B/2952